THE
MIND
OF
CHRIST

THE
MIND
OF
CHRIST

HAROLD A. BOSLEY

ABINGDON PRESS

NASHVILLE
NEW YORK

THE MIND OF CHRIST

Copyright © 1966 by Abingdon Press

Library of Congress Catalog Card Number: 66-10920

SET UP, PRINTED, AND BOUND BY THE
PARTHENON PRESS, AT NASHVILLE,
TENNESSEE, UNITED STATES OF AMERICA

To
The Annual Conferences
of Methodism in whose fellowship I have learned
much of the Mind of Christ

THE NEBRASKA CONFERENCE
THE BALTIMORE CONFERENCE
THE ROCK RIVER CONFERENCE
THE NEW YORK CONFERENCE

CONTENTS

INTRODUCTION

Renewal is one of the deservedly great words in the Christian churches today. It underscores a continuous need of men of faith. Treasured beliefs—in God, Christ, the Bible, the church—require steady attention and effort lest they become empty forms. The tragedy of the Christian churches today lies somewhere in this area: We have the forms of faith, but these forms have been emptied of powerful meaning by the erosions of time and simple neglect on our part. We still use the great phrases—"the Christian faith," "the Chris-

9

tian gospel," "the Christian witness"—but instead of girding us for battle they add to our despair. The profound meanings that created and made them things of power to move men's minds and stir men's wills have been slipping through careless fingers for several generations, and we find ourselves staring at them as rare museum pieces rather than finding in them guidelines for thought, resolve, and action.

That is why churches are seeking a renewal of faith on all levels of life and work; not, let it be emphasized, as an escape from the world of fact and challenge, but that we, as part of the church, may have something to say in our confrontations with and involvement in the world.

In The Methodist Church—to cite the one I know best—the thrust for renewal is many-pronged, reaching into liturgy, theology, ecclesiology, ethics, and, in these latter days, ecumenicity. The need for it has been pointed up by our apparent indecision, if not outright helplessness, as a church in one great conflict after another—in international affairs, the racial revolution, and the general crisis in morality. As one great problem after another burst from these areas, we found that we had little or nothing to say about them that was not found in the newspaper or other mass media. We reacted to these challenges, not as a self-conscious church fully aware of and fully committed to the Christian gospel, but as one among many institutions of our social order. We discovered to our dismay that we are not only a part of a culture pattern but are doubtful whether we have any identity apart from that culture pattern, and we have reacted accordingly.

But in and through what can only be called, in charity, the era of betrayal through conformity, prophetic voices and movements have kept the church from complete stagnation. To paraphrase Ezekiel, they have caused the church to know her sin. Their message has finally come through loud and clear. Judas betrayed Christ for thirty pieces of silver, says Matthew; the churches have betrayed him for something of comparable worth—the respect of the status quo! And the record of our betrayal is written in letters so large that he who runs may read.

Confronting the fact of war, did the churches immediately and unequivocally denounce it as evil—as a sin against God and a crime against man? Hardly. We wagged sage heads, furrowed learned brows, tapped purple-garbed breasts lightly in penitence, and spoke in measured tones of a "just war," a "necessary evil," and, when the spotlight of patriotic fervor fell on us, even suggested that war might be an instance of God making "the wrath of men to praise him!"

Even when Hiroshima lifted the evil of war to such heights that secular statesmen felt free to warn against its ever being used again, churches continued to form commissions to debate the pros and cons of the possible uses of the bomb! The schoolmen of the dark ages,

11

debating the number of angels who might stand on the point of a needle, have been joined by a considerable company of contemporary churchmen who profess to continue to find Christian reasons for engaging in war.

The churches' record on race relations is, if that were possible, even more tragic. While none—at least for several generations—have defended slavery as a Christian institution, a very large number have either fought for the retention of a social order divided along racial lines or have pled for the churches not to move "hastily" in their determination to remove every vestige of segregation from their own life, work, and structure, as a prelude to making this same insistence in social orders.

It is one thing—and justifiable—to take the necessary time for change by constitutional provisions in church structure; it is quite another—and beyond any justification—deliberately to exploit every possible constitutional evasion of the need for all possible speed toward an inclusive church. The deepest cleavage in the churches today lies in this area. It is a glorious truth that the most powerful voices and thrusts toward racial integration have come from within the churches. It is also true that the most tenacious and powerful social forces resisting integration have been found in or been nourished by the churches. The last stand of conservatism on racial matters is found in the white councils, the Ku Klux Klan, and in large segments of the churches.

It takes radically different forms in each place, but the end sought is the same: the retention of segregation in society.

But this schism in the soul of the churches has reached the breaking point in our day. If we are to hope, pray, and work for an inclusive church, we shall need a renewal in depth of our faith in why we do what we do.

We must ask whether the churches are ready for an effective role in the most profoundly revolutionary age men have known—an age when "the foundations are breaking up" for social orders, moral codes, and historic institutions alike. Are we so wedded to the forms of our faith that we have lost our capacity to see and to respond in obedience to the upthrust of new meanings in history? Or, to put it another way, are we willing to concede that the eternal meanings of our faith cannot be contained in the historic forms that have borne witness to them until now? If ever an age lived under the hammer of divine judgment in history, we are that age! And this judgment is beginning where it should—with the house of God.

But, and this is to arrive at the point with which we began, are we ready for "the living of these days?" I should think it axiomatic that we need a renewal of faith in depth if the forces of faith are to have a decisive effect in the course of life and events today or in the discernible future. There is only one place where, for Christians, such renewal can begin—by confrontation with Jesus Christ. There can be no significant renewal of the Christian church without a renewal in depth of our personal understanding of and loyalty to him. Without him the Christian tradition—theology, ethics, liturgy, and all else—makes little or no sense at all. With him, it is the only thing that does make both immediate and ultimate sense.

The World Council of Churches has made an important discovery of late. Rather, it has rediscovered something we should never have lost, namely, that we are bound together by one thing alone—our loyalty to Jesus Christ and his claim on us. He is our unity. He is what makes us one in a deep and abiding sense. Whatever hope there may be for greater unity among the scattered forces of Christendom lies in a renewal of our loyalty to him as the supreme loyalty of our life and witness.

It adds up to something like this:

If ever Christian churches are to recover a sense of mission, we must renew our loyalty to Jesus Christ.

If ever Christian churches are to achieve spiritual and temporal unity, we must renew our obedience to him as the Lord of our common life.

If ever Christian churches are to be a force for peace on earth and goodwill among men, we must be willing to "take up our cross daily"and follow where he leads.

The Third Assembly of the World Council of

14

Churches, meeting in New Delhi, put this discovery in the form of an affirmation which it commended to all churches for use in services of worship:

> We confess Jesus Christ, Savior of men and
>   the light of the world;
> Together we accept his command;
> We commit ourselves anew to bear witness to
>   him among men;
> We offer ourselves to serve all men in love,
>   that love which he alone imparts;
> We accept afresh our calling to make visible
>   our unity in him;
> We pray for the gift of the Holy Spirit for
>   our task.

The purpose of the meditations in this book is to make a serious and sustained effort to renew our understanding of him and to nerve ourselves to more complete obedience as his disciples in our time.

Chapter 1
WHY DID HE DO IT?

Scripture: Matthew 3:16-17; 4:1-11

Recently I came across a story that suggests the Christian strategy of renewal. A newly arrived missionary at a post in China asked a little girl who had been picked up as an orphan and cared for in the mission whether she had heard the gospel. "No," replied the girl, "but I have seen it." We are not so much trying to hear the gospel as to see it, and we join the company of those who through the ages have sought the meaning, purpose, and strength of their life in Jesus Christ. In doing this we step into the company of the

17

original group of disciples who tried mightily to learn his way of thinking, praying, and acting, hoping thus to become party to his power. Recall, if you will, the time they begged him, "Lord, teach us to pray." They were honestly puzzled when he, by his prayers, was able to help one whom they, by their prayers, had been unable to help. They asked, "Why could not we do that?" They had learned his way—at least the manner and verbal forms of his prayers—yet they could not do what he did. So they went to him for answer.

I

Paul, almost more than any other New Testament writer, stresses the urgent need for what can only be called a radically transforming relationship with Christ. And it is a many-sided relationship he describes. He urges his readers in the little churches scattered across the Mediterranean world to "Let the peace of Christ rule in your hearts," to "Let the word of Christ dwell in you richly" (Col. 3:15, 16). Over and over again, he prays that "The grace of the Lord Jesus be with you." He confronts the Philippian Christians with the direct challenge to "Let this mind be in you, which was also in Christ Jesus" (Phil. 2:5 KJV). Think of that as a pattern of renewal! The peace of Christ; the work of Christ; the grace of Christ; the mind of Christ! All these, says Paul, are the gift of fellowship with Christ.

Here we have the clearly stated yet always mystifying conviction that the Christian is one whose life has been caught up and transformed by the power of God found in Jesus Christ. "Paul in Christ—Christ in Paul" is the way Adolf Deissmann, one of the great students of Paul, sums up his interpretation of what it means to find and be found by Jesus Christ.

From Paul's day to our own, the Christian faith has been centered squarely, unshakably in Jesus Christ as the revelation of the will of God for man. We hold that in him God gets a firm and final grip on the minds and spirits of men. We believe that in him men find the will and feel the full power of the love of God. It is our hope and prayer that as we accept him as the Lord of our life we will become new creatures in him, that old things will pass away, that all things will become new, and, miracle of miracles, we shall become what we hardly have courage to utter—new creatures in Christ.

It is, therefore, a sound instinct that prompts us to take the long and arduous journey over nineteen hundred intervening years back to Jesus of Nazareth; back to the earliest records we have of his life and teachings —the four Gospels; back to the earliest interpretations of what it means to follow him—the letters of Paul; back to the earliest records we have of what the transforming power of Christ means in the lives of people like us—the book of Acts. By a legitimate union of

19

careful scholarship and sensitive imagination this not only can be done, but it must be done by Christians of every age. We, as it were, can visit the home in Nazareth in which he lived for all but two or three years of his life. We can stand on the banks of Jordan and hear God's call to the public ministry. We can join his disciples as they go on their slow journeys throughout the country; we even may dare to sit among them as he preaches the Sermon on the Mount.

But it will not always be quiet, tranquil, peaceful! We will be jostled by disturbed, suspicious, and angry men who seek to trip him up, to prove him a fool, a blasphemer, a subversive! As we go with him to Jerusalem we will sense both the exhilaration of Palm Sunday and the impenetrable gloom of Good Friday. And we shall probably take to our heels and desert him as did the rest of his disciples in that dark hour. But, by the grace of God, we may be gathered together —even as they were—by the risen Lord and hear the command to take his word to the ends of the earth.

The instrument I suggest we use in this venture consists of one word which will serve us as a probe in our search for understanding: "Why?" There is a time and place to center attention upon "what." What did he do? What did his critics say? What did his disciples say and do? Obviously, I will be doing that to some extent even as I try to concentrate on the "why" of it all. I want to ask and to find out, if possible, why Jesus did what he did, why some of his contemporaries listened to him, why a few believed while many doubted, why he forced a showdown on his critics and made it necessary for them either to accept him or to kill him. And, finally, again guided by the grace of God, I should like to know why he lived again—and lives eternally —in the human heart.

II

What Matthew Arnold wrote of Shakespeare is far truer of Jesus Christ: "Others abide our question. Thou art free." This underscores the need for genuine humility throughout our entire effort to renew and deepen our acquaintance with Jesus Christ. Yet the effort must be made if we are going to know him in a personal way. We shall be breaking through the surface of reported events in search of motives and causes both in him and in those around him. Any lawyer knows that this is one of the most essential yet most difficult of all undertakings. In spite of the doubts about and hazards of it, we must make the effort or surrender altogether all hope of vital, personal relationship with him. So long as men have purposes and motives that influence decision and action, we must try to find out why they do what they do, else we shall not understand them at all. And we need to understand Jesus Christ above all else.

Two general fallacies will haunt us as we engage in this effort to confront Jesus Christ. One bears the label of "fatalism." It asserts that he had to do what he did, that he had no choice, that he was little more than a puppet responding to the will of cosmic forces that were responsible for every move he made. The second fallacy bears the ominous word "impertinence"—and it does smack of impertinence to think we can ever fully understand the motives of anyone. If we are honest, we will admit the difficulty, if not impossibility, of ever fully comprehending our own motives and those of the ones we live with in love. How much greater must be the hazards of attempting to decipher the motives of one who lived so long ago and about whose life and teachings we have all too few records!

Strictly speaking, there is no full or ultimate accounting for anyone—except as God makes it. Gladly leaving that to him and his mercy, we nonetheless must raise such questions as will help us better understand Jesus Christ. That is modest enough, and that is the task at hand.

Let us center our attention upon his public ministry and ask, "Why did he do it?" Why did he leave his home and workshop in Nazareth—where he was sorely needed—and go off on a preaching tour? Why did he turn away from a quarter century of experience in the quietness and peace of his little community for what was destined from the outset to be a short, hectic, tragic life?

If we know our New Testament at all, we will surely

want to move carefully as we seek answers to these questions. This is what I mean: Mark, the earliest Gospel, begins with the public ministry and clearly gives the impression that Jesus began it under the direct influence of John the Baptist. On the other hand, John, written at least fifty years later than Mark, holds that Jesus knew all along that he was destined for the public ministry and that John the Baptist was but a minor factor in it all. Matthew and Luke wander indecisively between these two positions. All four agree that Jesus was called of God to the public ministry—and agreement on that is much more important than disagreement on the "how, when, where, and by whom" of it all.

Some of you may recall reading an article in *The Sunday School Times* years ago on this matter. It caught my eye and fancy in such fashion that I have never been able to forget it. That journal was the exponent of a thoroughgoing fundamentalism in all things religious. The author of this particular article, accepting the position of John that Jesus knew all along what was to happen, tried to imagine what went on in the mind of the babe in the manger. As nearly as I could make out, the babe was fully occupied anticipating the writer's own weird fundamentalist theological conceptions. In which case, he would have proved a doubtful savior of a needy world.

To those who say that he was born to it as a king is born to the purple, we must make reply: "He was born to certain things that must have prepared him to hear and to accept the call to the public ministry." We find these things in the experience of those who knew him personally and through whom we see and hear him.

III

To begin at the beginning in this listing of known and probable empirical facts about him, we center attention on the truth that he was born in and to a profound religious heritage and environment. In what we would call his cultural milieux, faith was the dominant fact and the knowledge of God was the supreme knowledge open to man, even as the worship of God was the most important act of one's life.

He was born to a heritage that spread before him a bountiful harvest of the human spirit. It all but idealized Moses. It exalted the prophets and priests of ancient Israel. It acquainted him with true hardship: slavery in Egypt, exile in Babylon, defeat and destruction on a dozen fields of battle. It was a heritage which celebrated the mighty deeds of God, the mighty men of God, the mighty movements of the will of God in the life of Israel—one which, in short, felt the purpose and the power of God in all that happened. A Jewish lad, nurtured on this heritage, would not understand our casual disregard of the reality of God. For him the

24

great fact of life would be: God within, God around, God below, God above—God all in all.

A heritage as such is an abstraction—and no child is born to an abstraction. He is born to a family and a community. Jesus came to a family and community in which this great religious heritage came alive in home, synagogue, and discussions at the workbench, the public wells, and the parks. The language of devotion which flows so naturally from his lips and spirit was a part of his life from infancy.

The synagogue meant as much to villages in Palestine as the church does to a small community in our time. It served as a school for the boys as well as a place of worship for all. It was no casual secular education which Jesus and his comrades received in the synagogue school; it was a thorough discipline in the teachings of the great rabbis who, for four hundred years, had been interpreting the meaning of the law as given by Moses.

Don't you wish we knew the names of the scribes and rabbis who taught our Lord in his youth? And if we did, would we not venerate them? For somehow they brought a deep and abiding love of God and trust in his will to birth in the spirit of Jesus of Nazareth. It is no accident that the first act in his public ministry was to go to the synagogue of Nazareth and there declare his call and commitment to the preaching of the kingdom of God.

We must not overlook another important part of

Jesus' birthright: the town of Nazareth itself. It was a city where freedom blew in every breeze. Why else was it suspect by the authorities of the temple in Jerusalem? It must have been the breeding ground of ideas reckoned to be dangerous. Why else did the Romans keep an eagle eye on it? And with good cause, we must admit. Nazareth was known as the hot bed of revolt and the caves in the hills of Galilee furnished all but impenetrable safety for robbers as well as rebels. In A.D. 6 Sepphoris, a city a few miles north of Nazareth, revolted against Rome—perhaps only gave shelter to some rebels—and Varus, the Roman general, leveled it to the ground. That was when Jesus was about ten years old—and I am sure he and his companions played among the ruins many times. It may have been there that he first got an inkling of the truth, "All who take the sword will perish by the sword" (Matt. 26:52).

All of this gives body and content to the proverb that was current in Jesus' day, "Can any good thing come out of Nazareth?"—a proverb that must have been coined and passed along by those who loved the status quo and wanted no critical breeze to blow upon it. But somewhere in his heritage, Jesus had been taught independence of mind, spirit, judgment, and life. Let us give Nazareth at least some credit for this.

Jesus was born to a troubled country and a people of divided counsels on what ought to be done. None liked their Roman overlords; all longed for the fast

26

disappearing days of freedom. But they were not of one mind as to what ought to be done about it. Some counseled, "Accept the Roman yoke—we've no choice"; others said, "Resist by any and every means and keep on resisting until we are either dead or free." Some counseled, "Let us wait for a heaven-sent Messiah to free us"; others called this hope a delusion. Some prayed for the coming of the kingdom of God by whatever means; others turned sadly away from this as a barren hope.

Sensitive boy that he was, Jesus must have felt—and felt deeply—the great spiritual tides that would flow in hope and ebb in despair, flow in great resolution and ebb in fear. He knew how great was the need for a deliverer—one sent of God who would bring peace, hope, light, and joy to troubled hearts and lives.

IV

Then came John the Baptist streaking like a heaven-sent comet across the sky of all Jews—including Jesus. He created as much of a stir in Palestine as Billy Graham has done wherever he has gone. Everyone went to see and hear him—even some Roman soldiers! Scribes, Pharisees, rabbis, the elders in Jerusalem—all went down to hear this desert prophet. And the common folk, too—Jesus among them.

At this point we encounter a puzzle in the records: Were Jesus and John related to each other? Only Luke makes the claim. The other Gospels make no reference to it. In fact, the Gospel of John is quite careful in its subordination of John the Baptist to Jesus. Apparently the Baptist had some hard-shelled followers in that early day who thought him superior to Jesus, else why would Jesus accept baptism at his hand?

In any event, Jesus was stirred to the depths by the message of John which was simplicity and forcefulness incarnate. "The day of judgment is at hand. It will be a day of punishment for sinners. Repent before it is too late. Be baptized and cleansed from your sins." And that is just what the multitudes did—Jesus among them —though the Gospels are careful to point out that he accepted baptism, not because he was a sinner, but in order to fulfill the scriptures!

Then came the call—the divine call—that gives answer to the question, "Why did he do it?"

There are some interesting agreements and disagreements among the Gospels on what actually happened that day when he was baptized in the River Jordan. Who heard the heavenly voice anyway? Everyone? Jesus alone?

Matthew thinks it was an experience that all could share. He writes, "And when Jesus was baptized, . . . behold, the heavens were opened and he saw the Spirit of God descending like a dove, and alighting on him; and lo, a voice from heaven saying, 'This is my beloved Son, with whom I am well pleased' " (3:16-17).

28

Mark, however, makes it a much more subjective experience, "And when he came up out of the water, immediately he saw the heavens opened and the Spirit descending upon him like a dove; and a voice came from heaven, 'Thou art by beloved Son; with thee I am well pleased'" (1:10-11). Luke goes along with Mark while John prefers Matthew's objective account.

All four agree that it was in this moment, though, that God made known to Jesus his will for his life henceforth. This was the dividing moment in the earthly life of our Lord—Nazareth lay behind; Jerusalem lay ahead.

Of this we may be sure: Jesus heard the voice because he was ready to hear it. It was the moment to which he had grown over the years in Nazareth. He was ready morally, spiritually, and intellectually for the experience which came upon him by the River Jordan. He was more than ready to hear the voice; he was ready to obey it. This reminds me of Christopher LaFarge's characters in "Each to the Other." A husband and wife had successfully evaded the responsibilities of parenthood and a significant home for years, thinking to postpone the day when they would be "thus tied down." Then came the day when she discovered that an unplanned pregnancy was in process. She hesitated about telling her husband but finally did so. He was quiet for a moment, then said, "This is the moment to which we have grown."

There are moments like this in the life of every person—moments to which we have grown; for which we are now ready; in which, by the grace of God, we can hear things that we simply could not hear before. Our Lord was brought to this point of maturity by his years in Nazareth, his sensitive and continual exposure to the religious heritage of his people, and every other factor that beat in upon him in the world in which he lived. He was ready for "the voice" when it spoke to him.

Certainly this experience placed a tremendous spiritual alternative squarely in the heart, mind, and spirit of a young man of thirty years of age. It is a tribute to his good judgment that he did not leap at it impulsively but looked at it carefully, turning it this way and that in search of hidden meaning. He knew he had a choice to make—one on which everything hinged. He knew that the choice once made could not be unmade.

That is why he went into the wilderness for an extended period of time, trying to think out what was involved. Can anyone misunderstand the questions that must have flooded his mind at this time? Could it be —could it possibly be—that he was the one appointed by God to be the long-awaited deliverer of his people? Is this what the voice meant? If it did, how much and what kind of power could he rely on? Finally, the hundred and one questions settled down to a gnawing doubt as to whether he was the Messiah, the one called of God to bring in the kingdom. Why not prove it?

His fears whispered, "Put God to the test. See whether he will support you in the work of the Messiah! You're hungry; you want food; see these stones? Ask God to turn them into bread. He can, you know; and he will, if you are his Son and especially dear to him."

When Jesus resisted this temptation, still another came—one born of his fear that he was too weak for the enormous task to be done by the Messiah. The tempter asked him to test God on this matter, too, to prove whether he would actually support him in a situation where his life was at stake. "Throw yourself off a high point and see if he will bear you up. If you are especially dear to him, if you are his Son in a special way, he will let nothing happen to you. And if he will not support you, you had better find it out now!" Still Jesus resisted.

Finally, the tempter played upon the human desire for security and promised our Lord the power to rule the world if he would forsake this mad dream of serving God and God only. Still our Lord resisted the temptation and determined to trust God and God only.

In the agony of the wilderness he learned and never forgot a lesson that some of us seem never to learn: We do not put God to the test. We do not because we cannot —and we cannot because the mind and the spirit of man cannot devise a true test of God's intention, will, or power. Actually the only way to test God is to trust him—beyond this we cannot go.

This is the answer which Jesus found in his ordeal of the temptations. He discovered that he must turn toward God utterly; that he must turn away from all else—family, respected leaders, and friends; that he must forsake every security which the world might offer him and choose God and leave the rest to him. This he did. And by so doing he inaugurated the great tradition of Christian choice which every man must make before he can become a disciple of Jesus Christ.

We are not born Christians. Nor can we continue as Christians simply by keeping our names on the records of churches. We must choose to become Christians. Every man on earth must be confronted with the call to serve him—this is the great commission of the church. And it is the most important choice a man is ever asked to make. Now, as then, it means that Nazareth lies behind and Jerusalem lies ahead; it means that the securities of this world are forsaken and the risks of serving God are embraced as a precious gift from him; it means that we are willing to become new creatures in Jesus Christ.

And we must be willing to hear that call—even as he was! It is more than simply the beginning of our ministry—it is our total ministry as Christians. It is more than our introduction to the church; it is the lifework of the church.

We who claim to be his disciples must take special heed of this firmness. We can speak in relative terms about our country, our denomination, our way of life, and even our standards of value. For there is opportunity for reconsideration and accommodation and prudent compromise in all these areas as they impinge upon differences of opinion. But we cannot afford to talk in relative terms about God's absolute claim on every human being and man's need to respond in absolute obedience. That claim is made through men neither better nor wiser than we are, but let us be clear on the point that we do not make the claim; it is God's claim; it is made on every man, and God expects an answer in full obedience of mind and will.

With Jesus, Paul, and other apostles both in New Testament times and throughout Christian history, we must be ready to do morally, spiritually, and intellectually all that must be done to hear, to heed, and to respond to the call to service in Christ's name. When that call comes, let no man ignore it. Rather let us do all in our power both to be ready to hear it and to have our children ready to hear it and be ready to respond in obedience to it. This is the most important single area of decision in a man's life. For the God of the universe is the God who calls, and the God who calls is the God who expects an answer—an answer from people like us!

Chapter 2
WHY DID THEY LISTEN?

Scripture: Mark 12:28-34

Text
"And the great throng
heard him gladly."
(*Mark 12:37*)

The Gospels assure us that Jesus received a large
hearing at various times in his public ministry. Several
very human and personal facts help us understand why
this was so.

I

The setting of his public ministry—his entire life,
for that matter—was in Palestine, if we may include
in that country, for the moment, a thin strip of territory
east of the Jordan River in which we find him upon

occasion. His public ministry began with a call from God at his baptism by John the Baptist. It lasted from one and a half to three years, falling between A.D. 26 and 29, so far as we can tell from the Gospel records which, of course, do not favor us with a precise chronology of events. All that is recorded in Mark might well have happened in little more than one year, whereas the events in John would seem to require at least three years.

Palestine—all of the Mediterranean world, for that matter—was under Roman rule, and the Jews were united only in their hatred of that regime. Tiberius was emperor in Rome, and he has a reputation among historians as a just administrator of the affairs of state. While the seams of the Roman state were to start opening soon after Tiberius' day, it was a sound ship through Jesus' lifetime. There is every reason to think that the Romans furnished Palestine with governors and procurators who were a cut above average in ability, because Palestine had a reputation for being one of the most unruly of Roman provinces. What the Romans scornfully called "religious fanaticism" lay at the heart of the unrest—witness the fact that it almost always burst bounds at the great religious festivals in Jerusalem.

Yet the Roman judgment on this matter cannot be taken without challenge. The Jews were intelligently as well as intensely religious. Of course, there were fanatics among them—witness the world-fleeing groups like the Essenes, about whom we have been hearing much these days in our discussions over the Dead Sea Scrolls. Strange prophets such as John the Baptist were likely to spring up at any time and set the country astir if not ablaze! Granting all this, the main tradition in Judaism exhibited an exceptionally high order of rationality. It revolved around Torah, temple, and synagogue as the earth revolves around the sun.

The Torah or Law was much more than the scrolls which contained the "Books of Moses" and later commentaries. It was Israel's answer to what moderns would call "the search for identity." The Law explained Israel to herself. The devout Jew found in the Law his reason for being as a person and as a people. It explained to him wherein he was alike and wherein he was different from other people. It alone enabled him to understand in measure, and accept in faith, God's dealings with men in nature and history. The respect accorded the scribes (students of the law) and the rabbis (interpreters of the law) by the Jew of Jesus' day speaks for itself. The Torah was more than a book; it was the voice of God to and for Israel—and every Jew grew up and grew strong in this faith.

A large and beautiful temple adorned the sacred hill in Jerusalem. Toward it the devout worshiper looked as he prayed, and to it he came as often as he could for the great feast days ordained by the Torah and celebrated in song and prayer. Not only priests and rabbis but ordinary people, too, such as Joseph and Mary and their family, came to the temple.

Coupled with the temple which, in Jesus' day, was the central symbol of the faith of his fathers—the cathedral, if you please—was the synagogue which could be found in nearly every village of any size in Palestine and throughout the eastern half of the Roman empire.

The synagogue served as sanctuary and school, a place of worship for all as well as a place where the men might study the law under the tutelage of the local rabbi or a visiting teacher. Judaism stressed the importance of such schools in the temple as well as the synagogues. Her greatest teachers were stationed in the temple and only the most promising students were admitted to their classes. This throws some light on Paul's ability—for he was sent to Jerusalem from the synagogue in Tarsus to complete his training under the temple teachers. The Jewish people were as carefully and as conscientiously trained in religious thought as a whole people could be. Consequently, anyone who presented himself to them as a religious teacher or prophet had his work cut out for him.

So much for the general background of the public ministry of our Lord.

There is no question at all about whether the people listened to him. When he came preaching, "The great throng heard him gladly," the record in Mark says.

And it is fully supported by the other Gospels. Crowds by the thousands pressed in upon him throughout the opening weeks and months of his ministry—and again at its close. They flocked to hear, to see, to touch him no matter where he was—in house or synagogue or at the edge of the Sea of Galilee. He was so jostled and pummeled by the throngs that he had to flee to the mountains to have time to himself. Even there, his disciples found him and reproached him for running away from the crowds.

As you would suppose, the political leaders of Palestine—Jew and Roman alike—took note of that fact and sent "agents" to keep track of what was going on. The religious leaders sent critics and hecklers to challenge and, if possible, to discredit him in the esteem of the throngs. The Roman officials made it a prudent practice to keep an eye on anyone who attracted much attention. He might be the source of real trouble. That the people in Palestine listened to him is so obvious that we must take it for granted. But why they did listen calls for a closer look at the facts and a careful listing of reasons.

II

The first fact is both simple and important. They listened to him because they were accustomed to listening to traveling preachers, teachers, and prophets. Every village had both a place—perhaps several places—and a time to hear such people. It was a public place where civil proclamations were read. It might be a grove of trees around the city well, or an open place beside the synagogue, or a park in the village square—as we would say—or the sloping shore of a lake. In any event, it would be much quieter than anything we are able to produce in a modern city where noises of every sort beat in upon us incessantly.

It was not sensational nor even unusual for an itinerant preacher and his disciples to come to a village and, while there, to invite everyone to gather around after a stop for rest and refreshments. Such incidents undoubtedly furnished a welcome break in the routine if not the quiet monotony of village life. There is no reason to think it was particularly hard for a preacher to get a crowd. Young and unknown teachers and preachers would be assured of a good initial hearing—after that, they were on their own if they should return at a later date.

It is a little hard for us to grasp the prevalence and the importance of the rabbis, the scribes, and other teachers of the law who loomed so large in public life in Jesus' day. Some of the teachers—the most famous— were attached to the temple in Jerusalem and, as a rule, stayed there. Others were more or less permanently stationed in the larger synagogues throughout Palestine. But many were on the move all of the time as itinerant teachers and preachers. Coming to a village, they would stay for a week or a month, interpreting the law, answering questions about it.

Actually, the scene in Palestine reminds a reader of medieval history of the travéling friars or teachers and preachers who roamed the paved roads as well as the forest trails of Europe for several hundred years. An even closer parallel is Wesley and his preachers moving from village to village in England preaching in churches, church yards, village greens, and open fields. It was all so amazingly informal—or "unstructured," as some might want to say! They would send word ahead that they were coming; meetings would be announced; the crowds would gather—and a church was born.

Some of you may have been thinking of one contrast between ourselves and the people of Jesus' day. They were trained to listen to long, involved, carefully thought-out discussions; we are not. If radio and TV presentations are valid indications of the kind of listeners we are—and I suspect they are about as valid as we can find—we either will not listen or we cannot because we have not been trained up to it. We seem to be doing better of late though. There was a time when we could roam the TV channels and radio stations from morning until night without once confronting a single challenge to serious, sustained thought and discussion such as the teachers of Israel served up daily in the public places of Palestine in Jesus' day. But now we are beginning to accept the discipline of sustained and hard thought on serious issues in an increasing measure in both radio and TV presentations, and this is all to the good. We may yet learn the discipline of sustained listening which the common people of Jesus' day had mastered so well. Their veneration of their great rabbis was so pronounced that someone has wisely observed, "No Hindu fanatic would more humbly bend before Brahmin saints, nor devout Romanist more venerate the members of a holy fraternity than the Jew his great rabbis."

III

We come now to a number of well-known reasons why people listened to Jesus: the compelling rumors, claims, and facts which ran ahead of him as he pursued his public ministry.

He was hailed as a healer, to state one of the most fetching of all these. This claim or rumor is guaranteed to get a crowd together any time, any place, anywhere —whether in Palestine in A.D. 27 or in Kansas, A.D. 1965 or in the famous Grotto of Lourdes, France, any time. The Gospels abound with healing miracles attributed to our Lord. Some of them also seem plausible in the light of our growing knowledge of man; others, quite frankly, are implausible in the extreme. Ours is not the first generation to be puzzled over what to make of them. Nor will we be the last. Several careful scholarly evaluations of the Gospel records of the healing miracles

41

are available for our assistance in this research. But, just now, it must suffice for our purpose to note that the claim was made that he was a healer and that people came by the thousands seeking his help. Two of the eight scenes from the Gospels which are dramatized in the beautiful reredos of the First Methodist Church of Evanston, Illinois, deal with healing miracles. And that is about the ratio of miracle stories to other material in the Gospels.

Strange as it may seem, the plain fact is that there was nothing unusual about the claim of miraculous healing in Jesus' day. It was made by many—not only by Jews, but by others in Greece and Rome as well. Shirley Jackson Case demonstrates the broad sweep of the claim in his book, *The Experience with the Supernatural in Early Christian Times*. It was an age of faith-healing and faith-healers. No religious leader could expect to gather and hold a following without being acclaimed a "healer" and providing some sort of demonstration of it.

Still another claim encouraged many to listen to Jesus: He was a former prophet come to life again— Elijah, or John the Baptist, or someone else. Such rumors, while immediately discounted by many, would draw others—how many we do not know. The Jews, like all other peoples, cherished the hope that their great leaders of yesteryear would live again to guide them out of present calamities. We do that even today.

42

In times of grave crisis we invoke the spirit of Washington and Lincoln, and, in a recent war, we read with fascination Vachel Lindsay's poem which told us that "Abraham Lincoln walked at midnight" brooding over the trials of his beloved land.

But the claim that really shook the ordinary citizen of Palestine loose from his plow or workbench or fishing boats was wrapped up in one word: "Messiah." That claim brought and held the big crowds we read about at various times in Jesus' public ministry. His was an age of eager expectancy of the advent of the heaven-sent deliverer of Israel.

Roman rule lay like a stifling blanket over the entire life of Israel. Though too powerful to be challenged, it was thoroughly hated. Dreams of freedom die hard—especially when the prayers lifted each Sabbath recalled the glories of the kingdom of David and God's promise to give the Israelites the promised land as their inheritance forever.

Jesus and every other new figure was certain to become the flaming center of this age-old hope and feverish expectation. He would be hailed as "Messiah" both by enthusiastic people who believed in him and by enemies who sought to get him in a situation in which he could be completely discredited or destroyed. For if a man who was accepted by the crowds as Messiah did not do what the Messiah was supposed to do, the crowds would turn and rend him—as they always do. But

43

whether the cry of Messiah was raised by honest belief or in malice, it was guaranteed to get someone—anyone —a big initial hearing.

We have in Acts 5 an interesting incident which throws much light on the commonness of the claim of Messiah in Jesus' day. Gamaliel, a teacher of the law and a member of the highest ruling court in Jerusalem, the Sanhedrin, begged his colleagues not to be unduly alarmed by the stir which the disciples were making by their preaching that Jesus was the Messiah and had risen from the dead. Gamaliel pointed out that shortly before Jesus two others were hailed as Messiah: Theudas and Judas of Galilee. He concludes by stressing the fact that after both had been killed their followers dispersed. This, he said, is what will likely happen again.

But it is enough for our purpose to know that everyone snapped to instant attention when the claim "Messiah" was made—the authorities as well as ordinary folk. It meant trouble for the Sanhedrin because the Romans demanded that they keep order in the temple and in Jerusalem on holy days, threatening that, if they failed to do so, the Roman legions would invade the sacred area and do it themselves. The claim "Messiah," meant one thing to the Romans: riot and bloodshed. But to the average Jew it meant a stirring of new life in the ancient hope of a divine deliverer. So, for various reasons, everyone was interested in it, whether it was made of Jesus of Nazareth or someone else.

"What of the claim itself?" you ask. "Did Jesus proclaim himself Messiah at the beginning of the public ministry?"

We cannot be certain of the correct answer. The Gospel records are far from clear on this point. He surely identifies himself with the work of the Messiah in his first sermon in the synagogue in Nazareth:

And he came to Nazareth, where he had been brought up; and he went to the synagogue, as his custom was, on the sabbath day. And he stood up to read; and there was given to him the book of the prophet Isaiah. He opened the book and found the place where it was written,

"The Spirit of the Lord is upon me,
because he has anointed me to preach good news to the poor.
He has sent me to proclaim release to the captives
and recovering of sight to the blind,
to set at liberty those who are oppressed,
to proclaim the acceptable year of the Lord."

And he closed the book, and gave it back to the attendant, and sat down; and the eyes of all in the synagogue were fixed on him. And he began to say to them, "Today this scripture has been fulfilled in your hearing" (Luke 4: 16-21).

Notwithstanding this obvious messianic beginning, Jesus at once warns his disciples not to call him "Messiah." Nor does he relent in this until the very last week of his earthly life, if then. We find ourselves face

45

to face with the fact that he thought himself to be the heaven-sent deliverer of Israel, yet he did not want that fact announced. "Why?" we wonder. Was he afraid of the misuses to which it would be put by the fanatics and the unscrupulous ones among the Jews? Did he want time to correct the weird, current misconception of what the Messiah would do before he accepted the claim *publicly?* He knew all too well what they expected— that he would come with legions of angels and overthrow the kings of the earth and make Jerusalem the capital of the world and make all other peoples subject to the Jews! He was not doing anything like that and guessed correctly that the crowds would turn away from him the minute they discovered it.

The facts seem to be these: The rumor or the claim that he was the Messiah was advanced early in his ministry and it brought crowds by the thousands. But when he did not fit their preconceived notions of what the Messiah should do, they lost interest. They rallied round briefly on Palm Sunday when the cry "Messiah, son of David," was raised for the last time. But when he again failed to live up to their expectations, they howled for his blood before Pilate.

IV

But there are other reasons why his contemporaries listened to him, reasons that lay greater claim to our attention today than the ones just mentioned.

To begin with, they listened because he was a great teacher. We have this on the testimony of even his critics. They said, "He spoke as one having authority." The soldier sent to spy on him brought back the report, "Never a man spake as this man." There must have been a directness, a winsomeness, a serenity, and power in his way of speaking to people. But, as his critics found out, he could speak with a fire that still crackles on the pages of the New Testament when occasion demanded it.

Most of his teaching was done in parables which were illustrations of great truths drawn from homely incidents in daily life and experience. What a keen eye he had for relevant detail! When a student of the law wanted to argue about the meaning of "Who is my neighbor?" Jesus told the parable of the good Samaritan. When Paul wanted to praise the love of God, he composed chapter 13 of I Corinthians; but Jesus told the parable of the prodigal son.

There is a fearlessness, a naked courage, about his teachings that commands instant respect. When the Pharisees brought the adulteress to him for judgment, they did not care a fig about the woman or her sins (She and her kind flourished in Jerusalem!); they wanted to trap him into an inconsistency that would discredit him as a teacher. He had preached forgiveness of sin—good. Moses preached the punishment of adultery by stoning to death. What shall we do with this woman: Obey Moses or you?

They got their answer—and what an answer! By all means obey Moses—stone her for her sin—only, "Let him that is without sin among you cast the first stone." That has kept sensitive Christians away from the ever-ready stone piles of the world ever since. But don't overlook the courage it took to beard those custodians of righteousness in their own den!

And it took just as much courage to challenge the principle of the segregation of the Jew from the Gentile, the righteous from the sinner—as Jesus did repeatedly. He not only called the outcast, Zacchaeus, down from his perch but publicly invited himself to dinner in Zacchaeus' house.

We must not overlook the great and quiet good humor—sometimes shading into gentle irony—that permeates much of his teaching. "What would you think," he asked the crowd, "of a fellow who would come to you with a plank in his eye and ask you for permission to take a splinter out of your eye?" He twitted the Pharisees, "You're hard to please! You complained because John the Baptist and his followers didn't eat but fasted. Now you complain because my followers and I do not fast but eat. You remind me of children playing the game of follow the music. The children who play the music complain to their playmates, 'We played music for dancing and you didn't dance; we played music for mourning and you didn't weep!'" How his listeners must have enjoyed that!

V

They listened to him—and we listen to him, too—because he spoke to the heart of every listener on the greatest themes that can engage the mind and spirit of man.

He spoke to every man as a man. While the rabbis and priests might and did talk about the law, the temple, and the Roman empire, Jesus spoke of and to "a certain man": "A certain man had two sons"; "A certain man was going down from Jerusalem to Jericho." It is quite clear that he was out of sympathy with all who separated religion from the life of people. He had sharp words for the legalist who exalted the law of Moses above the sinner, for the ceremonialist who exalted the ritual above the needs of the publicans, for the revolutionary who exalted freedom from Rome above the lives of the ones who would have to win it.

Jesus' teachings begin with and never leave a vivid sense of the concrete reality of the ones who were listening to him. They were human beings—his neighbors, friends, fellow workmen, fishermen, and hosts! And, as he spoke, they discovered anew that they were something more—they were the children of God and precious in his sight.

He spoke to them directly about the great themes

49

of God—his will and his kingdom; of man—his soul and his life here and hereafter; of the sins that separate us from one another and from God—and how to overcome them. Over and over again, as a mighty refrain he kept urging men, "The most important thing in the world is for you to know God, to love him, and to serve him with all your life." A sense of desperate urgency overwhelms us whenever we stop to think about what he says. He isn't trying to entertain us—not for a single moment. He is trying to persuade us to become citizens of the kingdom of God right now.

Jesus did not minimize the seriousness of what he was asking. In fact, if anything, he magnified it in every possible way. With a masterful use of hyperbole, he said he had come not to bring peace but a sword, to set father over against son and mother over against daughter—"a man's foes shall be those of his own household." He was trying to sting them wide awake to the urgency and the radical character of the choice he was asking them to make. He preached in a way that would have satisfied even Richard Baxter, who said a preacher must preach, "as a dying man to dying men."

Read the Sermon on the Mount again—slowly, aloud, thoughtfully, prayerfully. We will find ourselves looking at the stark outline of a wonderfully, radically, different life and world from the one we live in. We will discover ourselves to be under the judgment of the will of God; we will discover that our scale of values is hopelessly inadequate, that the loyalties of our life need both a new center and a new power. He tells us we can and must conquer greed, lust, anger, and hate. He tells us we can and must learn the ways of service, forgiveness, and love. One look at what Jesus wants his disciples to do "makes cowards of us all." Not because we disbelieve in a world where the love of God reigns supreme, but because we cannot recognize ourselves in it. But cowards or no—that is what he said to people like us who crowded around him long ago.

He was no world-renouncing idealist wanting to die. He was an idealist, right enough, but one who had unshakable faith in the guidance and the power of the love of God; who believed that, under God, we could do what God wants us to do, become what God wants us to be, and live as brothers, one of another.

The crowning point of his idealism is the realism with which he saw what lay ahead of all who followed him. It would be hard, too hard for words to carry the meaning. Denial, doubt, hate, ridicule, torture, death —all these and more, too—found their perfect symbol in the Cross. That, he said, is my way and it must be your way, too. Conquest of hate by love, of greed by service, of lust by sincere regard—all this begins as an inside job—something which happens within you. Then, and only then, can it become a power for the reconstruction of the world through what you do.

Would to God—his God and ours—that we in the

church that bears his name today were more aware of and further along on this inside job of being the ones through whom his words become incarnate—take on bone, sinew, heart, will, and idea! Conscious as we are of our unworthiness, limitations, and sinfulness, we cannot guarantee God or anyone else that we can do it —but we can guarantee that, to the best of our ability, we will try to do it in his name and for his sake.

Our Lord studies in principle every problem we face and he suggests an answer—God's answer. That, more than anything else, is why we, too, ought to listen to him today. Listen and not turn away, awaiting a more convenient season to declare our loyalty, or a less demanding leader. "Now is the appointed time." Now is the day of our salvation at hand.

Chapter 3

WHY DID SOME DOUBT?

Scripture: Matthew 5:38-48

Text
"You . . . must be perfect."
(Matt. 5:48)

When thirty years of age, Jesus of Nazareth was called
by God to leave his home, work, and family in Nazareth
to embark on a life of public ministry. The purpose of
the call and the ministry was both to announce—actually
to inaugurate—the kingdom of God and to urge men to
enter it at all costs. The public ministry was pathetically,
eloquently brief—lasting from one and a half to three
years, between A.D. 26 and 29.

I

There is no questioning the simple claim that many people listened to Jesus during the short, hectic, strenuous months and years he was going from village to village, province to province, and finally to Jerusalem. How many, of course, we do not know, and, beyond the numbers which came upon two or three occasions, the Gospel records afford us no basis for even an educated guess. It is quite clear that large crowds followed him during the early days of his ministry—some for healing; some to satisfy themselves as to whether he was the real Messiah; some, perchance, to hear him probe into the meaning and the mystery of God, man, and the proper relationship between them.

Whatever their reason, they came in large numbers in the opening days of the public ministry. While we hear of big crowds only occasionally, the Gospels furnish a vivid picture of people always around him, always listening as he went from lake shore to village to mountain top to city. There is reason to believe that he had some of his most intense audiences—in contrast to casual ones—during his last week in Jerusalem. It was at this time that many hung on his words—his disciples through love of him, his enemies with malicious intent.

It is important—but not enough—to note the fact that people listened to him. It is of even greater importance to confront and try to understand the further

WHY DID SOME DOUBT?

fact that, as we would put it today, "he could not hold his audience." Not that they literally walked out on him while he was speaking—there is no indication of that. But quite simply that they just did not come back once they got an idea of who he was, what he was saying, and what he proposed they should do about it. By the sacrosanct canon of "the voice of the majority" of his listeners, he was an unsuccessful teacher and preacher. One thing is quite clear: No pulpit committee would have looked at him twice! He was unable to hold his crowd—easily the most damaging thing that can be said about a Christian preacher these days!

John Masefield catches up the latent tragedy in this in some lines from "The Dream of Procula." Pilate is contemplating courses of action open to him as he thinks of Jesus of Nazareth and in the course of his meditation says,

> . . . This Jesus is alone.
> A common country preacher, as men say,
> No more than that, he leads no big array:
> No one believes his claim? [1]

Yet there are few facts in history harder for us to grasp than that, are there? It simply seems incredible that those who had an opportunity to hear him turned

[1] Reprinted with permission of The Macmillan Company from "Good Friday—A Dramatic Poem" by John Masefield. Copyright 1915 by John Masefield. Copyright renewed 1943 by John Masefield.

away. The irony of the contrast between then and now bites deep. He, who could not muster so much as a handful of disciples to see him die, now has nine hundred million souls who name him Savior and Lord, and who would be known—with what justice God alone knows—as his disciples. We need to ask and to try to find answers to the inevitable questions: "What on earth happened back there in Palestine between A.D. 26 and 29? Why did the overwhelming majority of all who heard him turn away either in active doubt or complete unconcern? In answer to the incredulous question, "Is it possible anyone could turn away from the opportunity to hear Jesus Christ?" history gives the even more incredible answer: "They did just that from one end of Palestine to the other."

Who are the "they?" you want to know. We find them in several groups so far as the records go: the militant nationalists, the special religious groups, and, then, the ordinary people. Each group had its own reason for doubting him and for drifting away from him to hear and, perhaps, to believe in "one who would come after him."

II

The militant nationalists rejected him because he did not believe in revolution and in the tactics of revolution as they understood them. This party or group carried a tremendous weight in Palestine at that time.

The entire country was a pot heated to the boiling point. One more burst of revolutionary enthusiasm and it would break into a racing boil. Jesus was well acquainted with this danger. How could he escape knowing of it when most revolutions and revolutionary activities centered in Galilee? While none broke into the open during his public ministry, they began to break out with increasing frequency and fury from A.D. 40. In A.D. 66 the great outbreak occurred which brought down the Roman fist with such vengeance that Jerusalem was utterly destroyed. All that led up to these later fearful events were in full operation throughout the lives of the ones to whom Jesus preached.

It is possible to single out two smaller segments of the militant nationalist group: the Zealots and the Sicarii. They might properly be called "the lunatic fringe" of the nationalist movement. Even so, they need to be studied at least for a moment because their activities seem to have precipitated the final fatal revolutions.

The Zealots were a small, fanatical, religious minority who believed that the Jews should revolt against Rome right away and keep on revolting until God in heaven would have compassion on their suffering and reward their devotion by sending them a Messiah backed by legions of angels. They were centered in Galilee and were all around Jesus during his lifetime.

57

He must have known many by name and must have heard them state their case many, many times.

The Sicarii—the dagger-men, the assassins—were the wildest, the most dangerous part of the Zealots. They were all for assassinating both the Roman rulers and anyone who cooperated with them. They would enter into a holy compact to kill the Roman leaders of some one village or area at the same time—much as John Wilkes Booth laid plans to have a wholesale assassination in Washington on the night that Lincoln was shot. As you would expect, the Romans erupted with the fury of Vesuvius each time such an attempt was made —and their wrath enveloped everyone much as the lava of Vesuvius enveloped Pompeii.

It was said of Demosthenes, the great Greek orator, that he kept saying one thing and one thing only to his contemporaries: "Let us march against Philip." Finally, they marched. In similar fashion—at least with similar intensity—the militant nationalists of all shades of feeling in Jesus' day put only one question to a new Jewish teacher or preacher: "Are you ready to lead a revolt against Rome?" They were ready to hail as "Messiah" anyone who said "yes" to this question—as several did both before and after Jesus of Nazareth. And when anyone would say "yes," they would rally around for another bloody assault on the nearest Roman stronghold.

They were not long in doubt as to how Jesus would

answer their question. When he explicitly repudiated the appeal to the sword; when he counseled reconciliation instead of retaliation—loving one's enemy instead of slaying him—the militant nationalists had had enough. They went away and never came back. They were waiting "for another."

Cannot you hear their comments as they left? "Another crazy idealist who does not appreciate the fact that the sword is the last word in realism." They may even have thought him a coward for counseling his disciples to love their enemies, to turn the other cheek, to "pray for those who despitefully use you." And, I suppose, by their standards he was an irresponsible idealist—may even have been a coward. They had plenty of reasons to doubt him.

III

It is hard in the space we have at our disposal to be fair with the reasons why certain powerful religious groups doubted and rejected Jesus. Yet we must make the effort or fail to understand what happened to those who listened to him.

The Essenes, about whom we are hearing a great deal these days as a result of their possible involvement in the Dead Sea Scrolls and manuscripts, were an influential group of religious folk who lived in or at the edge of the desert and in the caves around the Dead Sea area. They believed in separating themselves from the normal life and relationships of the world in order to be wholly dedicated to lives of purity before God. This they did by fasting, self-denial, and various rites for cleansing themselves of sin. John the Baptist may have been one of them—or at least deeply influenced by them. It was not unusual for one of them to present himself in a public place and issue ringing calls to repentance.

While we have no record of a direct encounter between Jesus and the Essene group, he may have been with or near them in the wilderness experience—perhaps in others. But there is little reason to think he was one of them, or was even interested in becoming one. He separated himself from the world in order to gird up his energies for a new assault on it. For this reason the Essenes—and anyone influenced by them—would doubt whether Jesus was a leader to follow and would turn away seeking another.

We are better acquainted with another small group of influential Jewish leaders who doubted him—the Sadducees. They lived in Jerusalem and were composed quite largely of priestly families of distinction and wealth. They were the distinctly elite or "upper crust" party in Palestine. They were led by the high priest and the supreme council, called the Sanhedrin, which was composed of some seventy-one elders in Israel. They were charged by the Romans with the maintenance of order in the temple area and were known as "the temple party." They were devoted to the Mosaic law and professed scant regard for the teachings of the later rabbis. They were dedicated to the temple as the dwelling place of the Most High. It is fair to say that the Sadducees regarded the Torah and the temple as the solid core of true religion. Righteousness for them lay in fulfilling the law. It was a matter of bringing the prescribed offering to the prescribed place at the prescribed time in the prescribed manner and having it received by the prescribed official and presented in the prescribed way.

It is not hard to see why the Sadducees turned away from Jesus. His scathing attacks on the over-emphasis on wealth, large contributions, and ritual correctness incurred their enmity. Nor were they passive about it. They did not merely avoid and reject him; they "sought a way to destroy him."

As we turn to still another group of religious leaders who rejected Jesus—the Pharisees—we shall want to proceed with great caution. It is easy to continue the ancient Christian practice of doing the Pharisees a grave injustice. Contemporary Christian scholars have gone a long way toward recovering a fairer view of the Pharisees and their contributions to Judaism. Without going into detail, we see one great fact which stands out: They were the authentic heroes of Judaism over a two-hundred-year stretch of tumultuous history. They had fought first the Greek, then the Roman effort to assimilate Jewish life and culture. They determined to die before they would forget or forsake their religious heritage. Nothing their foes could do—and they did all that mortal mind could devise—would break their determination. They fought for the faith of Israel not alone on the battlefield but also, and with greater success, in the areas of custom, food, clothing, and Sabbath observance. They believed in "total resistance" through "total obedience" to the law. They wanted loyalty to the law to permeate all areas of life, and they turned to the great scribes and rabbis for guidance as to how to do this. Righteousness, to the Pharisees, meant obedience to the law in the temple, at the table, on the street—at all times and places.

Understandably, they did not always agree among themselves as to what obedience to the law meant. In fact, they tended to divide into two general groups: conservatives and liberals. The conservative hung on the letter of the law, the liberal on the spirit of it. We get some notion of the strength—and, let it be noted, the weakness—of the Pharisaical position when we ask what it means to obey the commandment—"Remember the sabbath day, to keep it holy."

The rabbis brooded over what this meant in specific matters and came up with some interesting suggestions as to what might and might not be done in faithfulness to it. To the anxious wife (and, I am sure, even more to the anxious family) who wanted to know if she could cook food on the Sabbath, the answer came,

Cooked food may be cooked before the Sabbath (which begins at sunset) and kept on the stove, if the stove is heated with stubble or brush. If it is heated with wood, the food must not be put on it until the fire is cleared out or covered with ashes. (The idea is that the stove heated by wood retains its heat long enough to perform the actual work of cooking, which is not permissible on the Sabbath.) [2]

"What kind of work may one do on the Sabbath?" The rabbis answer this in detail.

How much must a man build to become guilty? Whoever builds anything, whoever chops a stone, strikes with a hammer or uses a plane or bores a hole, is guilty.

Whoever ploughs at all, or weeds, or clears away branches, is guilty. Whoever gathers wood, if it is to clear the ground, is guilty. . . .

Whoever writes two letters, whether with his right hand or with his left, whether he writes one letter twice or two different letters, or with different inks, in any language, is guilty.

Whoever writes two letters on two separate occasions one in the morning and one in the afternoon, is guilty.[3]

Here is an interesting suggestion!

[2] B. W. Robinson, *The Sayings of Jesus* (New York: Harper & Brothers, 1930) , pp. 79ff.
[3] *Ibid.,* p. 80.

A man who is overtaken by sunset while on the road must give his pack to a Gentile to carry. If there is no Gentile with him, he must put it on his donkey. As soon as he arrives at the first house or the first village, he shall take off such things as may be removed on the Sabbath; and as to the things which may not be removed, he loosens the ropes, that they may drop off of themselves.[4]

The conservative Pharisee insisted upon as literal a fulfillment of the law as possible—and in so doing was led to impossible extremes. The liberal Pharisee, well aware of this fact, tried to keep true to the spirit of the law.

It goes without saying that Jesus was at odds with the conservative position. His words brook no misunderstanding: Alas for you Pharisees who clean the outside of the cup and the plate while inside you are full of greed and evil. Clean first the inside and the outside will take care of itself. (Luke 11:39-40; Matt. 23:25-26.)

Yet Jesus had much in common with the liberal Pharisees—more than with the Essenes or the Sadducees. He shared their love of the law, their desire to serve God every moment of their life, and their interest in the spiritual renewal of Judaism.

But he could not imprison the free spirit of religion in any set of laws. He rejected legalism in any and every form.

[4] *Ibid.*, p. 81.

Paul had it right: "The letter killeth, but the spirit giveth life." (II Cor. 3:6 KJV) Jesus did not believe it possible to define righteousness—or God's goal for life—in terms of obedience to a law. "You must be perfect," he said—and I know of no more frightening statement in the New Testament. He is saying all too eloquently that God expects us not alone to fulfill the law, but to go far beyond it because no law fully comprehends the extent of God's will. Accepting the efforts of the scribes and Pharisees as the literal summit of great endeavor, he said to his disciples that what they did was good—but not good enough: "Unless your righteousness exceeds that of the scribes and Pharisees, you will never enter the kingdom of heaven" (Matt. 5:20).

And then—God have mercy on us!—he spelled it out! He extended the basis of discipleship to include motive as well as deed, intention as well as action, making it as evil to hate as to kill, to lust as to commit adultery, to covet as to steal.

While many of the greatest teachers of Israel would agree with Jesus' emphasis, the plain fact remains that most of them would not. The literalists and the conservatives carried the day in the ranks of the Pharisees, and they turned away from him. They saw correctly that Jesus' emphasis would finally break down their effort to make the Jews a separate and a peculiar people. They saw that religion, as he conceived it, was for all men as well as for Jews. They sensed in his understanding of faith a new form of assimilation of Jews by the rest of mankind until they were like everyone else. The Pharisees—conservative and liberal alike—were not willing to go that far. They, too, doubted and "looked for another."

IV

Now to the largest group of his contemporaries who turned away from him, namely, the rank and file of ordinary people. And there is no need to mince words about this. The casual listener thought him crazy; the thoughtful listener was frightened half out of his wits by what he was saying and doing.

Here is how it looked from where they stood: "He is undermining our religious traditions and institutions; he is challenging our respected religious leaders. He is an agitator, a troublemaker, and we are much better off without him!"

Put it another way: They doubted him for the same reasons that cause us to doubt him today. He asked the *unexpected:* "Go, sell all that you have and give to the poor!" He asked the *incredible:* "Love your enemies." He asked the *impossible:* "You must be perfect!"

He was not only the teacher of astonishing ideas like these; he was also a reformer, one who did many things that just weren't done. He taught forgiveness of sins—which was all right. But he had fellowship with sinners

66

—which was not all right. When he ate with publicans and sinners in direct violation of the accepted practices and laws of Israel, the average man was as shocked then as he would be now.

While the record is plain that he loved the common people and sought to help them in every way, it is also true that they did not return his affection and concern. They might hear him gladly—once or twice—but when he violated all their preconceptions about themselves, when he seemed to undermine traditional institutions and challenge accepted religious leaders, that was too much. He was going too far. They would not and they did not follow him. But they did not turn away quietly and look and wait for another. When their leaders gave the word, they turned on him like a pack of wolves and demanded that he be killed. It passes belief—but that is exactly what they did. They doubted him, rejected him, deserted him, and called for his death.

Our Lord ran head on into the nemeses of all religious prophets:

1) the love of the status quo
2) the dread of innovation
3) the determination to keep things as they are
4) the fear of change

He challenged the basic assumptions of the power structure in the civil and the religious life of Palestine, and he articulated his challenge on every level of life and by so doing triggered the deepest fears of the majority groups among his own people. This sealed his fate so far as they were concerned.

V.

Let us now strive to be honest with all who turned away from him in doubt. Do you not have the feeling, as I do, that we were there, too? Suppose he should come into our communities, into our churches, violating our preconceptions about ourselves, or races, our creeds, our ways of life—as he surely would. Suppose he should criticize our hallowed religious, social, and cultural ways—as he surely would. Suppose he should challenge the power structures in our churches, in our communities, in our country—as he surely would. Suppose he should start talking to us about the unexpected, the improbable, the incredible, the impossible. Suppose he should sum it up now as he did then: "You must be perfect!" Would we turn away doubting, looking for another? Or would we volunteer? If you think we would volunteer, would you not agree that we ought to do so in the spirit of one who hearing him said, "I believe; help my unbelief!" (Mark 9:24)?

Chapter 4

WHY DID
SOME BELIEVE?

Scripture: Mark 1:16-20

Text
"Follow me, and I will make you
become fishers of men."
(Mark 1:17)

It was a normal thing when people listened to Jesus—
so normal that it occasioned no question. His public
ministry fell in a day of many traveling teachers and
preachers—all of whom got a hearing. And when we
consider how quickly and how deeply he clashed with
what people expected and wanted, it is not surprising
that the overwhelming majority of his listeners did not
believe what he said and doubted every claim made
for him by his enthusiastic followers. If we are to look
for a miracle in this matter, it is that anyone believed

in him then or believes in him now. Yet some did and some do. In search of an answer to the "why" of this, we are thrown back upon the experiences of those who have believed in him in the past and those who do so today.

I

In this venture we turn, instinctively almost, to the New Testament. Where else can we hope for answers to who believed in him and why? The New Testament is a believing book, written by and about believing men and women. In its pages we discover a variety of beliefs and believers, fitful or half-believers, fearful believers, and some who tried to believe but found it difficult and gave it up. Yet, notwithstanding this variety, the New Testament is a triumphant record of the creative power of vital belief. It begins at a manger and ends fighting it out with the accumulated power of imperial Rome— and winning! So when we ask why some believed in him we are seeking the reason why the Christian movement grew so swiftly from a mere handful of persons to the world-girdling movement it is today.

We must, of course, begin with the disciples—there is no other proper place to begin than with those who knew him best in his public ministry.

Actually the four Gospels throw very little light on why the disciples chose to follow him. Matthew, Mark, and Luke sum up in a short paragraph the "calling of the twelve." Jesus saw Andrew and Peter fishing and he called, "Follow me, and I will make you fishers of men." Just that and nothing more! "Immediately they left their nets and followed him." Going on down the lake shore, he came to James and John mending their fish nets. They responded at once to his call to follow him. Some time later he saw Matthew sitting at his place, collecting taxes. To him he gave the shortest invitation of all: "Follow me"—and Matthew did just that. When, where, or how he came across the other seven disciples, the Gospels do not say—we literally stumble across their names as belonging to the twelve. I wish we knew more about the call of one, Judas Iscariot, but the records we have help us not a bit on this.

Luke, with his irrepressible love of the human touch which makes a good story, enlarges a little on the call to Peter, Andrew, James, and John. This is how he tells it:

While the people pressed upon him to hear the word of God, he was standing by the lake of Gennesaret. And he saw two boats by the lake; but the fishermen had gone out of them and were washing their nets. Getting into one of the boats, which was Simon's, he asked him to put out a little from the land. And he sat down and taught the people from the boat. And when he had ceased speaking, he said to Simon, "Put out into the deep and let down your nets for a catch." And Simon answered, "Master, we toiled all night and took nothing! But at your word I will let down the nets." And when they had done this, they enclosed a great shoal of fish; and as their nets were breaking, they beckoned to their partners in the other boat to come and help them. And they came and filled both the boats, so that they began to sink. But when Simon Peter saw it, he fell down at Jesus' knees, saying, "Depart from me, for I am a sinful man, O Lord." For he was astonished, and all that were with him, at the catch of fish which they had taken; and so also were James and John, sons of Zebedee, who were partners with Simon. And Jesus said to Simon, "Do not be afraid; henceforth you will be catching men." And when they had brought their boats to land, they left everything and followed him (5:1-11).

The Gospel of John comes up with an entirely different version of the calling of Simon. The first disciple, interestingly enough, was Andrew. Andrew and another (unnamed) person were disciples of John the Baptist when Jesus came by. They heard John say, "Behold the lamb of God!"—a traditional name for the Messiah. Immediately they left John and followed Jesus.

Jesus turned, and saw them following, and said to them, "What do you seek?" And they said to him, "Rabbi, (which means Teacher), where are you staying?" He said to them, "Come and see." They came and saw where he was staying; and they stayed with him that day, for it was about the tenth hour. One of the two who heard John speak, and followed him, was Andrew, Simon Peter's brother. He first found his brother Simon, and said to him,

"We have found the Messiah" (which means Christ). He brought him to Jesus. Jesus looked at him and said, "So you are Simon the son of John? You shall be called Cephas" (which means Peter). (1:38-42)

Jesus did not call anyone into discipleship until his public ministry was well under way. The great crowds were around, excitement was running high, and he was literally unable to be everywhere at once, as people seemed to expect. He needed help—right away. He sought out those who would drop everything, live with him, learn the good news of the gospel, get on fire with it, and spread out over Palestine as preachers and teachers. Every page of the New Testament indicates how heavily the disciples leaned on him at every turn. But they were not passive followers. They argued, scolded, begged, pled with him. They quarreled among themselves; they were rough with the little children who tried to push through the adults to get a good look at him. In and through it all, they tried to understand him, to grasp his purpose and power. When a parable seemed obscure, they asked him to explain it again—and he did. When he spoke of prayer, they asked, "Lord, teach us to pray"—and he did. When he chided them for their lack of faith, they came back with the humble yet spirited plea, "Increase our faith"—and this is what he tried to do on every opportunity.

Why did they believe in him? Why did they leave all

and follow him? Why did they court the anger of their families, friends, and neighbors, as well as the wrath of civil and religious leaders, by becoming and, with one exception, remaining his chief disciples?

While we devoutly wish we had more facts with which to work out full answers to these questions, let us prove true to the ones we do have—for they are of the utmost importance. We shall find them in the Gospels and in the sermons of the first Christian preachers as recorded in the book of Acts. Three terse statements of faith by the disciples themselves will serve us as good guides in our search for an understanding of why the disciples believed in him.

II

They believed in him because they thought him the long-awaited Messiah. Recall if you will how Andrew left Jesus at the end of the most memorable day of his life and, finding his brother, Peter, cried, "We have found the Messiah." Every disciple would say "Amen" to that statement of faith. Without exception, they believed him to be the long-awaited Deliverer and Redeemer of Israel, the one promised from of old by prophet and sacred scripture. Philip cried to his brother Nathaniel, "We have found him of whom Moses in the law and also the prophets wrote, Jesus of Nazareth, the son of Joseph." Nathaniel, when he saw Jesus, agreed, "Rabbi, you are the Son of God! You are the King of Israel!" (John 1:44-49)

There can be no doubt that Peter, the leader of the little band of disciples, agreed fully with Andrew and Philip that Jesus was the Messiah. Yet the word "Messiah" carried many meanings—some of which fitted Jesus, many of which did not. The disciples, in believing him to be the Messiah, thought primarily of the kingdom of God of which he spoke. They believed he was going to inaugurate a new order on earth—one in which God's will would be done as it was in heaven. They believed that he was the one who was to bring it in and to do so by the power of God. That is why they found it so difficult to face the fact of his defeat and death. Each time he brought up these grim facts one of the disciples would chide him about it—but he insisted that that was what was going to happen. And when it did, their fears mastered their faith momentarily, and they ran like rabbits for shelter and anonymity. But with his resurrection, all was changed. Their beliefs soared up again, and they preached him, as did Peter, as the long-awaited Messiah.

Peter makes two other affirmations of faith in Jesus Christ as Lord and Savior. On both occasions, though, he was speaking for other disciples as well as for himself; in fact, scholars are of the opinion that he is articulating the earliest credo of the Christian community.

The one occasion that comes to mind quickly occurred at the floodtide of Jesus' popularity. Jesus and his disciples were enjoying a brief period of quiet together on the shores of the Sea of Galilee. The disciples were excited about the crowds and were repeating what they had seen and heard said about him. Of course, Jesus was keenly interested in what people were thinking about him and wanted to know rather precisely what they were saying. Some said one thing, and some another. But Jesus did not leave the matter there—he never did. He asked his disciples to become more than carriers of tales of what other people believed. "But who do you say that I am?" he asked. According to Matthew, Peter answered, "You are the Christ, the Son of the living God" (16:16). Mark has Peter giving even a shorter answer, "You are the Christ" (9:29). Luke has the shortest answer of all: "The Christ of God" (9:20).

While the Gospels do not enlarge on what Peter had in mind as he said this, his three sermons in the opening chapters of the book of Acts give us a much more complete picture of his meaning. Confronting the very ones who killed Jesus, and standing on the steps of the temple itself where he had stood with Jesus many times, Peter made several points about the meaning of Jesus Christ: Jesus was the servant of God; he was the one foretold by Moses and the prophets; he came to save us from sin and death; you killed him, but God raised him from the dead; repent of your sins, accept him as the Messiah, and follow him before it is too late.

That is what we might call the motif or the theme song of the New Testament and the early Christian church.

The third affirmation of faith in Jesus attributed to Peter is closely akin to this and is found in the Gospel of John. (Actually it is John's equivalent of the great confession of faith we have just been studying.) As the story of it develops in John, Peter made this confession under the grave pressure of actual division within the fellowship of those who had been following Jesus. John calls all who followed Jesus "disciples" and speaks of "the twelve" when he wants to single out the chief disciples. The trouble arose when many of Jesus' disciples objected to something he was saying, so much so in fact that this is what happened: "After this many of his disciples drew back and no longer went about with him. Jesus said to the twelve, 'Will you also go away?' Simon Peter answered him, 'Lord, to whom shall we go? You have the words of eternal life; and we have believed, and have come to know, that you are the Holy One of God'" (John 6:66-69). The very phrase "the Holy One of God" is a Messianic title and Peter is saying in effect, "We have come to know that you are the Messiah, the long-awaited Deliverer of Israel."

As the disciples lived with him and learned from him, they were weaned away from the usual notions of what the Messiah was to be and to do. They believed he would establish the kingdom of God, not by overthrowing the

77

political organization of the world and recentering it in Jerusalem, but by actually inaugurating a new relationship with God. They believed that in and through him God was inserting himself in life, in history in a new way—so radically new as to bring one age to an end and to inaugurate another. The old had passed away and all things had become new in and through the coming of Jesus Christ! They believed he had delivered them from the gravest foes man faces—not the Romans —but sin and death. They believed that the kingdom he inaugurated had behind and within it the power of God and that nothing could prevent its coming in full force in human life. They believed it their call to preach the gospel; to leave all and follow Jesus Christ. They believed that in him man finds God.

But the disciples—these men who came to be known as the "pillars of the church"—were not the only ones who believed in Jesus Christ. I've already mentioned the half-believers, fearful believers, and those who finally gave up on it.

Among the half-believers we find the scribe who, hearing the parable of the good Samaritan, exclaimed that the neighbor was the one who helped the injured man. To him Jesus said, "You are not far from the kingdom!" How I wish we knew what the scribe said and did then! Did he draw back from the shining vision that drew Peter, John, and the others on to immortality? He must have—at least we hear nothing more of him. Let us hope he never forgot that moment—when he was so near the kingdom, yet so far from entering it.

Another like him is the rich young ruler who had kept the law, yet was haunted by a deep sense of something missed. He asked Jesus about it and learned that he lacked one thing. Think of it! Just one thing—most of us lack a long page of things! But when this fortunate young man heard what it was he lacked, he went away sorrowing. He, too, stood, but hesitated, on the threshold of the kind of belief that would have transformed him, along with the fishermen and tax-gathers, into a disciple or a missionary. But when he turned away, he walked straight off the pages of history and left it to others to write thereon their lives.

I cannot list those who were tempted to believe without recalling the spies sent by the priests to catch Jesus in some sort of blasphemous utterance in order to discredit him as a teacher. But these spies came back with the staggering report that "Never had they heard a man speak as this one did!" Needless to say, they got a good dressing down by their employers for it. But they must have been moved by the glimpse of the glory they caught as they joined the ones around him and heard him talk of the way of God and the ways of men. We lose track of them at once—being practical men they wanted to keep their jobs, I suppose, so they spoke no more of this young teacher who for a moment had lifted them to a new plane of understanding and appreciation.

As we think of the half-believers, we must recall John's report on the disciples who left Jesus because they were offended at what he was saying. Give them credit—they believed in him up to the point where he shocked their reason and shook their traditional beliefs too hard. It was fine for him to say that he was the Messiah—but when he seemed to identify himself with God, when he seemed to make light of Abraham, that was too much. They walked out on him. But do you suppose they could ever forget him? When he was killed, what did they think and say? Could they ever forget those long evenings with him when the kingdom of God hung as low as the stars and as full of hope as the full moon in the Palestinian sky?

There must have been a considerable company of true believers in addition to the eleven disciples. When Judas deserted them, they cast lots between two men, Justus and Matthias, to decide which one of them would take Judas' place. Both of them were loyal believers and worthy to become one of the twelve. The book of Acts speaks of the "twelve" calling the whole body of disciples together, and in this number were men like Stephen, Philip, and others who soon were to preach the gospel to all who would listen.

In this number, too, were the faithful women, who seemed always to come up at the right time—as is the way of faithful women in all ages!—his mother, Joanna, and Mary the mother of James and many others, including Mary Magdalene, who could never forget how her life had swung from darkness to light when he said, "Neither do I condemn thee! Go and sin no more!" She had done more than obey him; she had followed him. She was among those who, brokenhearted, went to the tomb to prepare his body for burial, only to find that he was not there! If we are going to have saints at all, I am glad she is one of them!

They were all together in the upper room on Pentecost—disciples, the twelve, the faithful women—in a rich community of faith when the great impulse came, like tongues of fire, sending them to the ends of the earth. Who was there? Among them may have been Mark, Stephen, Philip (who was to convert the queen's treasurer), and the brothers of Jesus. No sooner had they taken to the highways of the Roman empire than they were joined by men such as Paul, Apollos, and others who shared the task. Together they were the first generation of a company of the faithful whose members were to swell until today they number nine hundred million and include you and me.

But what was it they believed about him? To put it in a very simple and direct word (which theologians may enlarge upon in many ways) they believed that they had found God in Jesus Christ, or that God had found them in Jesus Christ. And to that tremendous

81

affirmation of faith the entire Christian tradition shouts "Amen."

III

We believe in him today because we have found him to be our clearest revelation of the will of God for the life of man.

To say this is but to echo one of the deepest continuing convictions of the Christian tradition. One of the most reliable scholars of our day writes, "Jesus Christ is 'final' in this sense—that the nearer we get to him, the more we know him, the more truth and reality we find in his yet unexhausted revelation." This statement, I believe, can be translated into everyday vernacular in some way as this: Jesus Christ faced in principle every problem that we face and has suggested answers that are truer than any other answers we know anything about. But we must put him to the test of faith and work.

After we make due allowance for the fact that all such statements about Jesus Christ come from men who are already his followers, I do not see how we can avoid the conclusion that those who follow him find him to be the peerless leader of the human spirit as it keeps pushing beyond the frontiers of what we think and know. The very unity and power of the Christian witness on this point is as complete a demonstration of truth as we can ever hope to get outside the area of mathematical proof itself. For wherever we turn in the Christian tradition, we find men aware of the fact that Jesus Christ has set before us certain "open doors" into more abundant living; doors which, being opened by God through Jesus Christ, cannot be closed by man; doors through which none can force us against our will and choice; doors beyond which we glimpse a portion of "The house not made with hands, eternal in the heavens."

The longer we study him, the better we know him; the more honestly we try to follow him, the more certain we are that to know Jesus Christ is to know God. This is not an irrational conviction, an item of blind faith, bolstered by nothing but the necessities of dogma. The reasons for this provide an actual embarrassment of riches. Let me sketch them in two short paragraphs.

Jesus Christ saw more deeply into life than any other man. He saw:

> All its lights and shadows;
> All the wealth and all the woe,[1]

saw it with clear eye, considered it with a fair mind, and identified himself with it from top to bottom. He lived no sheltered life. His discoveries about God and man came the hard and high way of daily experience. He seems to have met every sin of which we are capable in those few tense years of his life. He met the material-

[1] Alfred Tennyson, "Idylls of the King."

83

ist who thought he could put spiritual food in barns. He met the hypocrite who prayed in public so men would think him devout. He met bitter, angry people and people whose lives were dominated by fear and hatred. He met people who had surrendered to the lust for money, power, and sensuality. He knew all too well of people in high places who failed to do their duty—and the innocent had to suffer. Crowding in upon him were the multitude with tarnished souls and dimmed ideals—the ones in whose lives there was a great emptiness, a spiritual vacuum. He knew what was in man—then and now—let us make no mistake about that!

He went among men, throwing open the door to a new life. "You are the child of God," he said to his way-lost generation. "God is seeking you in love, as a shepherd seeks a lost sheep. He wants to give you another chance at the full life you are missing. He wants you to know the meaning of peace, joy, and usefulness. Put first things first—put him first, and you will be on your way toward a new life. He will help you each step of the way. Through difficulties, failures, dangers, even death, you can count on him. He will not leave you comfortless."

The story of what happened has gone to the ends of the earth, moving men as no other story has ever done. Many of his hearers turned away, but some believed and followed him and in so doing ushered in a new day for mankind. The sinner arose determined to sin no more. The materialist reversed himself and learned how to give, to share, to sacrifice. The hypocrite dedicated himself to learning a new prayer: "Lord, be merciful to me, a sinner." People found their bitterness, anger, fear, and hatred melting away when exposed to this message of the love of God. He revealed, as no one else had ever done, the divine depth in common things. Even the lilies of the field blossomed to the glory of God when he passed by. The tired mother's heart leaped high when he beheld intimations of the kingdom of Heaven in little children—the very ones who made her house noisy and her day a long stretch of hard work! The unwilling tribute of the soldier still stands: "No man ever spoke like this man!"

Is it to be wondered at that he who opened the door to a new life for so many people should himself become the symbol of new life to all who through the ages have come to know him? That is precisely what has happened. "You have the words of eternal life," cried Peter. "Behold, old things have passed away; all things have become new," exclaimed Paul. Two hundred years after Jesus' death, a disciple, Irenaeus by name, exultant with renewed life, could only say, "He brought everything new by bringing himself." From our own day comes the testimony of a great English thinker, John Caird: "He is the light of all our seeing." Explain it how you will, theologically, the plain historical fact must be faced that, in him, God was working a mighty work of redemption in human life and history through the experience of men like us.

He opened the door to a new life. He became the symbol of new life. And the gospel, the good news, to our generation is this: That door is still open! Enter it and you will find God, and in finding him, you, too, will find new life—life with strength, courage, joy, peace, and purpose.

One of the most amazing things about all this is to discover how alive it is today! I think of Paul standing on Mars' Hill proclaiming the gospel among the many statues that could be seen in every direction as he stood there. The story of that little episode in Christian history was little more than a page in a book for me until I stood on Mars' Hill recently and got the feel of the place where it happened. Then I realized how impossible, incredible, it must have sounded to his listeners! I no longer wondered that they laughed at him! For he was an itinerant preacher standing up among the great symbols of six hundred years of glory—and bringing that glory under judgment—the judgment of God. I am sure Paul was lucky that he secured the continuing interest of at least two from the crowd who heard him upon that occasion.

Living as we do, with the great symbols of Baal and all the materialistic urges of man around us, do you think for a moment that we will get a hearing in the

86

presence of our symbols of materialism? I do not know what the ultimate answer to that is, but I do know what our immediate responsibility is: We had better try! We had better put our every energy into getting a hearing. The task we face today cannot seem any more impossible than the one which Paul faced so long ago. But if we believe as he did that Jesus Christ can transform life, can give new courage, can give a new sense of direction, can reveal new meanings for life and history, then we have a gospel to preach that must be preached and will be heard.

Not long ago someone asked me how many members we have in the church of which I am pastor. That was easy to answer so long as we were talking in terms of round numbers. I could say, give or take a hundred, we have about fourteen hundred members. But the one who was putting the question persisted, "How many of them really believe in Jesus Christ?" I did not have the answer to that one for the good and sufficient reason that fourteen hundred other persons besides myself *were the answer*. I kept wondering what the fourteen hundred members of this church would say if they were approached individually by someone who asked of each one, "Now tell me, who do you think he is?" I wonder what the cumulative answer would be. Whatever it is, that is the answer we are trying to make in and through the witness of our church today.

Whether we are standing on Mars' Hill actually or in

imagination, trying to recapture what Paul said, or whether we join gladly with the Christians of our own life and time and make our confession of faith, each man must formulate and make his own personal confession of faith.

So far as I am concerned, the one drawn up by the Third Assembly of the World Council of Churches in New Delhi and transmitted to all Christians continues to be a reliable guide line for thought and action today. This is what we are trying to say from the many Mars' Hills of the twentieth century:

> We confess Jesus Christ, Savior of men and the light of the world;
> Together we accept his command;
> We commit ourselves anew to bear witness to him among men;
> We offer ourselves to serve all men in love, that love which he alone imparts;
> We accept afresh our calling to make visible our unity in him;
> We pray for the gift of the Holy Spirit for our task.

May God grant us the faith and the courage to say "Amen" to that—and both take our place in the great tradition of those who believe and give it to our children as our most precious possession.

Chapter 5

WHY DID HE
SEEK A SHOWDOWN?

Scripture: Matthew 23:23-39

Text: "O Jerusalem, Jerusalem,
Killing the prophets and stoning
those who are sent to you! How often would
I have gathered your children together as a hen
gathers her brood under her wings, and you would not!
Behold, your house is forsaken and desolate."
(Matt. 23:37-38)

The four Gospels give us not one but several portraits of Jesus Christ. And I doubt not that if other Gospels had been preserved and admitted into the New Testament canon, we would have still other notions of him. It is easy to understand why this is so: The Gospels were written by different men at different times and places with somewhat different sources at hand and quite different reader-audiences in mind. Each writer was convinced that he had some authentic new insight into the life and teachings of our Lord. Then, all felt as Luke did: "It seemed good to me also, having followed all things closely for some time past, to write an orderly account" (1:3).

Common sense as well as critical scholarship bears out this approach to the humanness of the reasons for writing the Gospels. And it is a shame to lose this human touch in a mistaken desire to surround the records with a supernatural sanctity. There is sanctity enough in their humanity. The writers were not writing for the fun of it. Nor were they trying to make a name for themselves as professional writers by producing a "best seller." They were trying to set down as fully and as accurately as possible "the greatest story ever told."

Matthew and Luke had Mark before them. They respected it enough to follow it carefully, but they were not satisfied with it. If they had been, they would have settled for it and not written the Gospels that bear their names. But they had other material which they thought important and true; therefore, they added it to Mark at the appropriate places. The same is true of John, who seems to have had Mark and Matthew before him —perhaps Luke. He had something new he wanted to add—and he did.

I

Against this background, it is easy to see why and how different views of Christ might creep into the Gospels, one presenting him one way, one another. For example, there are some incidents which caused a seventeenth-century dramatist, Dekker by name, to describe Jesus in these lines: "A soft, meek, patient, humble, tranquil spirit, the first true gentleman that ever breathed."

The only thing that is wrong with this view is that it is all wrong. Such a man as Dekker describes is never surrounded by a mob screaming for his blood, condemned by religious authorities as blasphemous, and crucified by political authorities as a menace to public order—a subversive, we would say. Yet all this happened to Jesus of Nazareth during his public ministry. There must have been more to him than is found in Dekker's lines or in the children's hymn about "Gentle Jesus, meek and mild."

That his public ministry was brief, hectic, tumultuous, and destined for a tragic end is a matter of public record. But why did it happen that way?

The answer to that one is easy! It happened because he sought a showdown, demanded a decision wherever he went and of whomever he met. His teachings throb with an unmistakable urgency, with a call to immediate decision and vigorous action. His very first word in the public ministry, according to Mark, sounds the tocsins:

"The time is fulfilled, and the kingdom of God is at hand; repent, and believe in the gospel" (Mark 1:15).

91

Similar urgent warnings abound throughout the Gospels:

"He who is not with me is against me" (Matt. 12:30).

"No man who puts his hand to the plow and looks back is fit for the kingdom of God" (Luke 9:62).

And the one saying repeated six times over in the four Gospels is the most disturbing and radical of all:

"If any man would come after me, let him deny himself and take up his cross and follow me. For whoever would save his life will lose it; and whoever loses his life for my sake will find it" (Matt. 16:24-25).

Urgency to the point of simple impatience runs like a scarlet thread through all his teachings. He is one of the original "men in a hurry!" He does not say, "Take your time—think it over—and let me know what you decide to do." Rather he says, "Choose, choose—and choose right now." It reminds me of that far-off day when Antiochus Epiphanes, heading the Greek forces, met the Roman legions in Egypt and the two commanders had a conference before battle. Antiochus Epiphanes wanted control of Egypt, but he did not want to do battle with the Roman legions to get it. He asked time to think it over. The Roman commander took his sword, drew a cricle in the sand around the Greek leader, and said, "Decide before you leave this circle." I am sure those who listened to Jesus with any degree of care understood exactly how that Greek commander must have felt!

II

But, you ask, why all this hurry? Why did he seek this showdown at the heart of Israel's life? He sought it in the synagogue—but why? Because he believed that the spiritual leaders, the scribes and Pharisees, were misrepresenting the law and leading the people away from the kingdom of God. Believing this, he challenged them in the name of the great prophets, in the name of God himself, to seek the kingdom of God with all speed. He insisted that they dig beneath the surface of the law and discover and be led by the spirit within it. And when they refused to do it, he called them "blind leaders of the blind"; he likened them to those who "scour the outside of the cup but leave the inside unwashed"; he called them "whited sepulchres, serpents, and brood of vipers."

I find myself wondering if Thomas Dekker ever read those words! I am sure the scribes and the Pharisees heard them and "took offense" and labeled him an enemy.

He sought a showdown in the marketplaces of Palestine as well as in the synagogues. Here he found men so absorbed in the things of this world that they had lost touch with the things of God. They were slaves of convention, custom, and tradition. Some had lost God completely, save for an inner spiritual emptiness that haunted them. Others had the wrong approach to God, thinking that the fanfare of trumpets and a big offering in the temple were enough.

Jesus would have none of this—and he could not keep quiet in the presence of it. He brought their entire way of life and worship under judgment as being utterly inadequate. Like the Pharisees, they "took offense" and turned away looking for those who would save their souls by salving their sins.

Jesus sought a showdown in the deadliest place in all Israel to seek one: the temple itself. He sought it in the very temple where as a boy he had heard the learned doctors discuss the law. How many times he visited the temple during his public ministry we cannot say with accuracy. But we can say with confidence that every recorded visit was the occasion for a clash with the priests or the Sadducees, who watched over the temple. Jesus believed that for many priests and people alike the temple had become a substitute for God. What was intended to be a sacred place where men might meet God had become an actual barrier between man and God. Therefore, standing within the temple and perhaps eyeing the priests themselves, he said, "Woe to you blind guides." And then like a prophet of old, he described the way in which they had been perverting religion.

When, upon occasion, his disciples were asking him to admire the beauty and the strength of the temple buildings, he was not impressed. He said, "There will not be left here one stone upon another, that will not be thrown down." (Matt. 24:2) Standing with them one day on the Mount of Olives across the valley from the temple, he burst out in the saddest words Jerusalem ever heard: "O Jerusalem, Jerusalem, killing the prophets and stoning those who are sent to you! How often would I have gathered your children together as a hen gathers her brood, and you would not! Behold your house is forsaken and desolate."

III

Thus the records run: He sought a showdown, demanded a decision at every level of life, because he believed the kingdom of God which he was inaugurating involved all of life. And, as all men must, he sought the showdown within himself, first of all. He asked, "Am I ready to serve the kingdom of God?" His entire life as well as his public ministry pivoted on this question —and he knew it. He sought the answer in the wilderness and through the temptations. The question haunted him then and—as all great questions do—time and time again even after he had found the answer to it. Later in the public ministry, his disciples urged him not to go to Jerusalem, where another and possibly fatal clash with authority was all but inevitable. They wanted him to stay in Galilee, where he was out of the reach of the outraged temple party. The temptation to do this must have been very great, but he threw it off and went to Jerusalem for that final showdown. Once there, the question came up again in the Garden of Gethsemane, where in grave agony of spirit he found himself all but unwilling to go ahead; he found himself wondering whether he was ready for the awful tomorrow that even then in the person of a search party was coming across the valley to arrest him. Luke catches the desperation of decision in his word, "And being in an agony he prayed more earnestly; and his sweat became great drops of blood falling down upon the ground." (22:44) When he had won the victory, he awakened his sleeping disciples with words wrought out of his own experience, "Rise and pray that you may not enter into temptation." (22:46)

He sought a showdown, demanded a decision of his disciples and of all would-be disciples, not once but many times. His call to them was brief to the point of being abrupt: "Follow me and I will make you fishers of men." He never made it easy for them. None could complain at the end of his public ministry that he had lured them into discipleship by false promises of ease and glory. "Foxes have holes, and the birds of the air have nests; but the Son of man has nowhere to lay his head" is the way he greeted two who said they wanted to follow him. (Luke 9: 58) How is that for an invitation to discipleship? It breaks every rule we know today for making friends and influencing people, but it told the honest truth about what lay ahead of him in his public ministry. He expected it, too, and wanted as disciples only those who, knowing it, were still set on coming.

Once he had selected his tiny band of a dozen men, he poured out his time and efforts on them without stinting. He taught them the meaning of his mission; he kept going over the meaning of the kingdom of God with them. He tried to nerve them for the final bitter hours when it would seem as though every power on earth were arrayed against him and them—and they had been abandoned even by the power of heaven. It must have been a hard thing for him to discover that they could not keep watch with him for an hour in the garden, that they scattered in all directions when he was arrested, that only one—if one—was close enough to see him die.

He sought a showdown with the Sanhedrin in the temple in Jerusalem because he wanted to carry the challenge of the kingdom of God to the very top of the hierarchy of religious leaders in Palestine. He was not content to dispute with the lawyers and the scribes in the villages of Palestine—though he did this. He wanted to go to the very center of the spiritual life of Israel— the temple—and there confront the chief priest and his associates, as Nathan of old had confronted David, and say, "Thou art the man!"

And, speaking in all reverence, he seems to have sought a showdown with God himself on the cross. How else shall we interpret the terrible query, "My God, my God, why hast thou forsaken me?" It was bad enough to be ignored by the crowds, disowned by the religious elite, deserted by his disciples, but to wonder whether he had been forsaken by God—that was to fill the cup of suffering to overflowing. Thank God, he got a full answer to that one as soon as he asked it! Then he could say—and somehow we feel the deep inner peace of it all: "Into thy hands I commit my spirit."

IV

But why all this? Why did he seek this all-inclusive showdown of everyone everywhere which led to the cross?

Three things must be said in answer to that, the first of which is almost a truism: Jesus was not simply a teacher and preacher of righteousness; he was a prophetic reformer, a man called to action by the voice of God, and he had to obey God rather than men! What he was talking about was more than a new idea to be thought about; it was a new way of life to be lived. It demanded decision, sacrifice, and action. He did not get into trouble with people when he preached that they should forgive the sins others committed against them—they had heard that many times before and considered it good doctrine. But when he actually had fellowship with sinners; when he flung wide the door of discipleship to them; when he ate and drank with Zacchaeus and welcomed Mary Magdalene into the company of those who gathered around him and his disciples—that was going too far.

Too far for them, perhaps, but not for him. He was trying to change life, human relationships and institutions. You do that as you get actively involved—not by standing on the shore and waving your arms, but by plunging into the water. Like the prophets before him, he wanted to know who was for him and who against him in all this. He believed in it himself. He had chosen it to do. He had the right to ask others to choose —and he did—and he does.

Don't feel sorry for those who get involved and get hurt—even killed—in the battle against sin and evil! Let us save our tears for those of us who refuse to get involved, who draw back at the point of decision and sacrifice!

A second reason why he sought a showdown might be phrased this way: He believed himself to be the one through whom God was bringing the kingdom of God into human life and affairs. Therefore, it was his duty to present and to explain it to everyone—to make it real, as real as he could. This is what he did—and with an urgency which did justice to the nature and importance of the kingdom. What he was saying was most urgent!

99

The way we say a thing will depend in large measure on what we want to say. If I should see a lovely sunset and want to call it to your attention, I would say, "Look!" in quiet hushed tones—perhaps with only a voiceless gesture—because that is the nature of a sunset. But if I saw a runaway car heading for an unobserving pedestrian, I'm afraid I would shout a warning at the top of my voice because of the radically different nature of the situation.

I hope I shall never forget the stinging rebuke Dorothy Sayers gave the clergy some years ago: "You have the greatest good news on earth—the incarnation of God in human life—and you treat it as an insignificant news item fit for page fourteen of the chronicle of daily events!" And she's right, isn't she? We do have the most sensational news in the world—news that never grows old—yet we treat it as though it were so well known as to be a hackneyed item of faith!

Jesus was convinced that what he was telling people was the most important thing they would ever hear, also the most urgent. It just would not have made sense for one who believed what he did to go about tapping people on the shoulder and saying, "Don't look now—and don't get excited—but this world as it is is coming to an end. You had better get ready for the new one God is initiating before your very eyes!" If you believe so important a thing as this, you will not be able to keep the note of urgency out of what you say. The most important thing in the world must be said in the most urgent manner possible—and this Jesus did.

The new kingdom which he felt God was inaugurating was to be radically different from any known kingdom—it was to be a kingdom of love. It was not to be a sovereignty of power as were the kingdoms of the Pharoahs and Caesars, but one of love, one in which the measure of greatness would be the number of men served, and the one acclaimed greatest would be servant of all. That this kingdom would call for a radical criticism and overhaul of all of life goes without saying. That service in the kingdom would be difficult and the applications for admission to it would be few were equally apparent.

"Enter by the narrow gate; for the gate is wide and the way is easy, that leads to destruction, and those who enter by it are many. For the gate is narrow and the way is hard, that leads to life, and those who find it are few." (Matt. 7:13-14)

Jesus knew that men could not be herded into the kingdom like sheep into a sheepfold; he knew they must enter freely, willingly, from choice, and with at least some knowledge of what they were doing. But he believed that the decision for or against the kingdom was the most important one before every man—thus the urgency with which he presented it. When the lifeboat is pushing away from a sinking ship, a person either gets in it or stays behind. It was this kind of decision Jesus felt was before men. That is why he forced a showdown of all who would listen.

I have been describing how he sought a showdown. Now I am wondering whether that is the right way to put the matter—at least as far as he was concerned. Did he seek a showdown, or did the showdown seek him? He felt and knew that something tremendous, something of immeasurable proportions, something far bigger than he, was happening to and through him. Eternity was battering down the walls of time. God was knocking down the walls of man's conceit, pride, self-sufficiency, and self-righteousness and was giving him another chance to live as a son of peace and righteousness.

When Jesus heard the soldiers coming across the valley to arrest him, he may have felt as Thomas à Beckett did when he heard the footfalls of the approaching assassins: "Those feet have been pursuing me over the years; now they have come—and it is good." Thus the Cross becomes a blazing symbol of what it means to live and to die for God's sake. And as the song most of us learned in childhood has it:

> Must Jesus bear the cross alone,
> And all the world go free?
> No, there's a cross for everyone,
> And there's a cross for me.

V

It is a sorry thing when we who call ourselves Christians flinch from the showdowns that are inevitable to the proclamation of the kingdom of love in a world like ours. Can't we see, can't we feel deep within us and all around us that something bigger than ourselves, something more lasting than the world, is hammering away at the walls of this world as it is? Hammering, hammering by night and by day at every level of our life, knocking our little kingdoms of power, pride, and wealth into cocked hats? Can't we see that it is our clear and simple duty once more to demand that men choose for or against God and his kingdom of love as we see them in Jesus Christ? Just as Jesus saw that the deepest problem of his day was not the Jews against the Gentiles, but God against man as he was, can we not see that the deepest problem of our day is not the free world against communism or east against west, or one race against another, but God against us all as we are? God has all of us by the scruff of our prejudices, fears and hatreds, and he is saying in no uncertain terms, "Learn to live with each other or else!" And that "or else" crackles loud with the doom to the listening ear of a poet like Hermann Hagedorn in *The Bomb That Fell on America*.

I wish I knew the answer to this one: Do we as churches have the courage of our convictions to force a showdown at every level of life in the name and for the sake of the kingdom of God? If I did, I would feel con-

103

siderably easier when we settle down to hammer out policy statements at our conferences and board meetings. I keep asking myself, "How are we going to approach our task of framing basic policy for Christian churches in these desperate days? Are we going to lift up the highest ideals of our witness and lay plans to achieve them with all possible speed, letting nothing hinder? Or are we going to enter into the usual nice calculation of all of the fears and prejudices which bind and blind us and finally seek only to maintain the status quo?"

I think I know what I in my better moments want to do, but I keep asking myself whether I have any right to speak in a representative capacity for the rest of the church. So I must ask my fellow churchmen: What do we want the church to be—a conservative or a progressive factor in society? Is she supposed to find and embrace the least offensive position on all controversial issues, or is she supposed to carry on in the high tradition of those who look to God rather than to man; who say, "We must obey God rather than the Gallup Poll?" Suppose church conferences take a vigorous forward looking position on these matters: What will we do? Walk out because our ideas have been passed over, because our prejudices have not been heeded? Or will we stick with the church and try to find our way in her will?

It has been my privilege to share in the last two General Assemblies of the World Council of Churches, and in each of these we have passed great resolutions as to what churches could and should do for world peace. But I bow my head in humility and shame when I ask what these resolutions have meant to the local churches. How have they been received in various countries? We need to know; and the answer, I fear, is being written in terms of positions taken by churchmen all over the world.

Here in this country the National Council of Churches has taken an aggressive leadership in this matter of realistic thought and action in behalf of world community and world peace. It has placed all churches —Protestant, Roman Catholic, and Jewish alike—in its debt by its vigorous leadership.

Yet on the local level we have done so very little, haven't we? We have been afraid to launch out on the peace programs and the proposals of the World Council or the National Council or the General Conference lest we be misunderstood by our communities, our nations, and our neighbors. We have been afraid to force a showdown, to demand a decision first within our own common life, then within the society and community in which we live, and finally within the world itself.

This is no time for calculated timidity to pass as Christian discipleship. If we are afraid to force a showdown now on the great issues of our day, we will never find the courage to do it later. And as we fail—if we fail—I can all but hear from him under whose uplifted hands we now bow these words: "O church, church, killing the prophets and stoning those who are sent to you! How often would I have gathered your children together as a hen gathers her brood under her wings, and you would not! Behold, your house is forsaken and desolate!"

Chapter 6
WHY DID THEY KILL HIM?

Scripture: Matthew 26:57-68

Text
"They answered,
'He deserves death.'"
(*Matt. 26:66*)

They killed him! "Brightest and best of the sons of the morning"—they killed him! They made him die the death of a disobedient slave, a rebellious citizen, a public menace. Not for him the clean, quick, merciful death of a brave man and a soldier, but the shameful, public execution of the cross. Even before they wounded and killed his body, they had lied about him, mocked him, spit upon him, received him with blows, made him the object of public derision, paraded him back and forth in the city three times to the tune of jeering mobs, and finally made him carry his own cross as far as he was able. When he broke under it, they picked out a husky bystander to take it the rest of the way. When they got to the top of Calvary, they killed him. They nailed him to the cross and after three hours of agony he died.

I

The recent Vatican councils have faced the problem of who was responsible for the death of Jesus. Yet there is little room for doubt as to the proper answer. At the time he lived, the Jewish high court was forbidden by Roman law to exact the death penalty for any crime no matter how serious it might be. Only Rome could exact that penalty. Therefore, Rome, in the person of Pilate, was responsible for the actual execution of Jesus. But what shall we say of those who brought him to Pilate on a trumped-up charge? Are not they, too, deeply involved in the guilt of his execution? Not their descendants to be sure, much less the Jewish people as a whole, but the ones who actually did it? There was guilt enough to go around for all who were there upon that fearful occasion: Jews, Romans, and the disciples who deserted him in his hour of need.

"But why did you kill him?" is the question which we must ask of the ones who did it. We must turn to the Romans and Pilate, to the Sanhedrin and the chief priest, to the mob, to Judas Iscariot, and finally, to the ordinary people of Palestine, and put that one question to them: "Why did you do it?"

Interestingly enough, the facts in hand suggest the answer which each one might make to our query. Beginning with the soldiers who actually put him to death and working backward and outward from them to the mass of ordinary people themselves, we can get a fairly clear picture of why they killed him. The Romans involved would give quick answers. The soldiers who did it would say, "We were on the execution detail that day. It was our duty to crucify the ones sentenced to that punishment. We were not responsible for the orders; we only carried them out." So far as I can see, we have no moral right to criticize those men—at least, so long as we expect soldiers to obey orders. That is part of a soldier's duty and life. He who didn't obey orders would be a poor soldier.

But when we turn to Pilate, our troubles begin and keep pace with his. It is hard to make up our mind about him largely because the four Gospels do not give us a clear picture of him and his relationship to the trial and execution of Jesus. They agree on a number of things:

1. Pilate conducted a hearing for Jesus and his accusers, the priests of the temple.
2. Pilate found Jesus not guilty of any charge worthy of discipline, let alone the death penalty his accusers were asking.

3. Pilate tried to free Jesus three times but was dissuaded by the howls of the mob.
4. Finally he gave in to their request to crucify him.
5. He made it plain that the responsibility for the execution lay with Jewish, not Roman, law.

Some years ago a distinguished British lawyer defended Pilate's action. Recalling the fact that Pilate was operating under Roman law, applying it to a country so addicted to uprisings that it was really in a state of military occupation, James Stephens wrote,

Was Pilate right in crucifying Christ? I reply, Pilate's paramount duty was to preserve the peace in Palestine, to form the best judgment he could as to the means required for that purpose, and to act upon it when it was formed. Therefore, if and in so far as he believed in good faith and on reasonable grounds that what he did was necessary for the preservation of the peace of Palestine, he was right.

A noted American correspondent interviewed one of France's most distinguished colonial administrators and found him very sympathetic with Pilate. He felt that Pilate was quite right in executing Jesus as a measure of public peace. His only criticism was that Pilate did it in Jerusalem at the Passover; he should have arranged to have it done much earlier in Galilee.

Pilate would agree with these men, I am sure. He would say that he killed Jesus in order to prevent many

110

others from losing their lives in a riot or, worse still, open uprising.

What shall we say of Pilate's reason—and the reasoning of those who support him? Pilate was not a weak ruler—but he was a prudent one. His reputation as an efficient governor was at stake. He had to do a good job in Palestine in order to get into a better responsibility in Africa, or Greece, or Gaul. More than he liked to admit, his reputation rested on what people like the chief priest in Jerusalem thought about him and his rule. Several of his predecessors had lost their jobs because Jewish leaders had appealed to Caesar for their removal. All this was in Pilate's mind as he faced Jesus and his accusers on that dreadful day.

Pilate's cardinal mistake lay in not making a firm decision as soon as he heard the case and determined that Jesus was innocent of any charge he could entertain under Roman law. He should have thrown the case out of court at once and warned the Jewish leaders to keep such complaints within their own courts. Instead of acting vigorously and swiftly, Pilate hesitated—and he who hesitates in the presence of a mob is lost. Spurred on by the priests, the mob demanded the death of Jesus—and no substitute which Pilate could offer would satisfy them. Finally, in order to keep the peace and to keep his record clear of complaints, he gave the order which, translated into the language of the creeds, has given him fearful immortality: "Suffered under Pontius Pilate, was crucified, dead, and buried."

II

Now we are back to the chief priest, the Sanhedrin, and the mob with our question: "Why did you kill him?" Let us begin with the mob. Mobs are as pathetic as they are vicious. In them a man loses his status as a man and becomes part of a wolf pack. He doffs his individuality and personality and dons the shameful moral anonymity of the lowest form of human life, and surrenders to the lowest form of human behavior.

And when the mad fit is over and the daylight of reason begins to filter through his consciousness, he creeps off into the darkness of obscurity and shame. Ask the mob why they wanted Jesus' blood and they would have mouthed the words given them by the priests: "He has sinned against our holy law. He deserves to die. We want to protect the faith and institutions of our fathers which he threatens. That is why we want him killed." But if we could lay hands on any one of them as he sneaked away home when it was all over and ask, "Why did you kill him?" he would doubtless have answered, "Who, me? What makes you think I had anything to do with it?" It is useless to question a mob, so let us turn to the ones who are really responsible for setting and keeping in motion the chain of events which culminated in Calvary—the priests of the temple and the Sanhedrin—or such of its seventy-one members as were there at that time.

Jesus had had several serious open clashes with temple authorities before they arrested him. The chief priest discovered him preaching in the temple early in Holy Week and demanded to know by whose authority he was preaching there. The chief priest had a point. Only one who had sought and obtained permission of temple authorities could do that. Mark's record of the event is plain, "And as he was walking in the temple, the chief priests and the scribes and the elders came to him, and they said to him, 'By what authority are you doing these things, or who gave you authority to do them?' " (11:27-28) Jesus replied with a sharp parable which stated in no uncertain terms that his authority came from God and that he did not propose to let them review his credentials. Mark continues, "And they tried to arrest him but feared the multitude, . . . so they left him and went away." (12:12) But they had to get rid of him—that was clear enough. His insubordinate attitude could not be tolerated! So they tried to trick him into a treasonable utterance by asking him whether they should pay taxes to the hated Roman government in the form of a tribute to Caesar. But he did not fall into this trap. So they set others for him. Finally they decided to arrest him by night, bring him in for a secret hearing at the home of the high priest, get some evidence against him through cross-examination, and then turn him over to Pilate and ask for execution. Their guards, led by Judas, found him, made the arrest, and brought him in for questioning. This was not a legal trial—it was more like a hearing. If ever a man faced a packed jury, Jesus did! He had no friend in the room. So far as we know, not a voice was lifted in his defense.

When morning came, a semblance of a trial was held in the temple, the charge of blasphemy was shifted to the charge of treason, and he was taken to Pilate for trial and sentence. Conscious of the weakness of their case, the authorities took along a crowd to shout for the right thing at the right time.

As we see the council in session in the temple, we can detect a number of different reasons why various ones in it might have wanted him out of the way:

The priests—because he did not recognize their authority in the temple; the ones who had the concessions in the outer courts—because he had ruined their business by creating a fearful row four days before and might do it again; the scribes—because he seemed disrespectful of the law; the Pharisees—because they were smarting under his denunciations. All had something against him; but they did not need to kill him! They might have kept him in protective custody until the Passover was over and then sent him home with a warning. Yet, to them, death seemed the only sure cure.

The Sanhedrin had a just cause for wanting him out of the way, though they may have "felt" it rather than seen it clearly then. They were committed to institutions and courses of action which tended to separate Jews from Gentiles and keep them forever apart. They declared immediate and unrelenting war on every effort that went against them. Whether they sensed it or not, this was precisely what Jesus was doing in his teachings and life. He became the highest common denominator of our differences—the one in whose sight and service we become one. This emphasis in Christianity has been vigorously rejected by Judaism from Jesus' day to our own. I mention it now lest we fall into the easy habit of saying that those who rejected him then did so in ignorance; that now it would be different. I doubt that. I am of the opinion that he would be rejected by everyone and every group that prides itself on its separateness from the human family for whatever reason—whether Jew or Gentile, white or colored. Just as even the liberal Pharisees were glad to get rid of him then, so would they and their spiritual kinsmen in other areas of life today. Jesus moved in the ancient prophetic tradition of proclaiming the brotherhood of man. Partisans of any form of separatism will always resent advocates of this. They would crucify Jesus as quickly today as they did then—and by the same proceedings, with mob fury thrown in for good measure.

115

III

It is a sad thing to ask Judas Iscariot why he wanted to have Jesus killed: sad for him and sad for us. Judas seems to have felt that Jesus betrayed him and the other disciples about the Messiahship. Apparently Judas kept hoping that Jesus would drop his passive role and revert to the older notion of what the Messiah would do, namely, overthrow the oppressors of Israel. Instead of facing them with power, Jesus was facing them with weakness. Instead of founding a glorious new kingdom he—and they—were destined to find an inglorious grave. Judas' disillusionment was complete when in the Last Supper Jesus made it plain that his public ministry was nearly over, that he would be killed, and that they would have to carry on with only his spiritual presence. That was thin gruel after the rich hopes on which Judas had been nourishing his spirit. His entire being revolted; he left, and threw in with the ones who were seeking Jesus' death. All he did—and it was enough—was to lead the temple guard to Jesus' resting place outside of the city and identify him to them.

Judas is a living example of how quickly love turns to hate if love feeds on selfish ambition and dreams of personal glory. Instead of blaming himself for misunderstanding Jesus—as the other disciples did—he blamed Jesus for misleading him and thought he deserved death for it. I have no desire to add a word of

116

condemnation to Judas for what he did; I very much doubt whether a word could be added, even if we were minded to try.

IV

Now to the public with our question—to the ones whose lack of interest, whose refusal to believe and to follow him sealed his fate and delivered him helpless into the hands of those who wanted his life. Why did they not so much kill him as stand aside and watch while others actually did it? There must have been tens of thousands of them lining the streets and the roadways on that fearful day when he was dragged back and forth across the city three different times for trial, exhibition, and execution. I might as well confess that I find it easier to understand those who sought his life in malice than those who stood idly by thinking it an affair of little importance. If the rank and file of his contemporaries had been really interested in him, his enemies would not have dared lay a hand on him. How well they illustrate the plain fact that the gravest and most common sin of good people is not lurid wickedness, but passing by on the other side! They will never know what they missed. They could not feel the tragedy of his death because they had missed the glory of his life. And if we could get their attention long enough to put the question, "Why did you let them kill him?" we would want to be braced for the answer: "What is all the fuss about? He had it coming. He criticized our leaders. He questioned the value of sacred institutions. He condemned our morals, our ways of living, and even our attitudes toward others. He violated the basic canons of good sense, good taste, and sound morals. We are better off rid of such."

The late Richard Roberts of Canada had the right of it when he asked if there might be some other way to deal with a rebel such as Jesus than to kill him. It is confession of callousness, blindness, and invincible stupidity simply to snuff out the life of anyone who makes us miserably uncomfortable. I hope we will not flinch when we call Jesus a rebel. How can we call him anything else if we are careful to understand what we mean by it? The late Albert Camus, brilliant French thinker, addressed an important volume to answering the question, "Who is a rebel?" One of the most helpful parts of his answer is the assertion that a rebel is not someone who is merely saying no to life as it is or things as they are. Rather, he says no to something, refuses to accept it, because he says yes to something else of greater importance. A rebel is "A man who says yes from the moment he makes his first gesture of rebellion." Jesus was a rebel in this sense: He said no to life as it was because he had first said yes to life as God intends it to be. He said no to the kingdoms of this world based on

naked power because he had first said yes to the kingdoms of God based on love. He said no to our darkness
and yes to the light of the love of God.

Over the last year, the play and now the book, *The
Deputy,* has been creating a great deal of discussion not
only in this country but abroad. The theme of the
book and the play is well known and the universal
moral problem in them is the one we have been talking
about: Do good people have a moral right to keep quiet
in the presence of evil, or must they speak up and speak
out regardless of the consequence?

Lest we think this purely a matter for examination in
the behavior of the Roman Catholic Church during the
persecution of the Jews under Hitler, I call your attention to a book, *Thirty-Eight Witnesses,* by A. M. Rosen-
thal of *The New York Times.* This is an incredible,
unbelievable recital of how thirty-eight human beings,
the silent neighbors of a young woman, stood by and
watched her being stabbed to death in three separate
attacks over thirty-five minutes rather than raise an out-
cry lest they get involved in the situation. They kept
quiet; they played it safe; they stood to one side while
the great and grave tragedy was being enacted.

Who can forget—or bear to remember—Edmund
Burke's most famous line: "All that is required for the
triumph of evil is that good men remain silent and do
nothing"?

V.

Now to the most difficult place of all to raise the question—the throne of God himself—and to ask, "Why did you let us kill him?"

Who can bear the answer he might make?

"I knew of no other way to do it. I did not want him to suffer and die as he did. I did not want you to neglect, misunderstand, and finally kill him. But I knew of no other way to let you know the full meaning of my love for you except I send one whose life was the full and perfect embodiment of it. I hoped you would receive him with rejoicing and follow him with adoration. I created you so you might do that. You are free moral agents: free to believe or to doubt, to affirm or to deny, to follow or to refuse, to love or to hate, to preserve or to kill. Such freedom is necessary to you, to your life as I want it to be. It is your greatest danger, too. You can misuse it—and in the misuse of it someone always gets hurt. You could not truly obey my Son unless you were free to disobey him; you could not truly love him unless you were free to hate him; you could not really follow him unless you were free to kill him. I knew the risk of it all when I made you that way, but I never knew how dangerous a thing it was until I heard him cry out to me, "Why hast thou forsaken me!" Then I knew, as never before, the inescapable tragedy, yet the glorious necessity, of your freedom. And when his heart broke, so did mine—and so must yours if ever you are to understand my love for you. You see, you not only killed him in A.D. 29 on Calvary outside the city wall in Jerusalem— you have done it many times since. Every high hill in the world is a candidate for Calvary. And you—even you who put the question to me—know you would do it again if he were to come among you as he did among them."

To which there can be only one response: "God be merciful to me, a sinner." Or perhaps, by his mercy, "Lord, I believe! Help thou my unbelief!"

They killed him in order to silence him—that is clear. But were they successful? All history shouts the answer to that.

By what right do we propose ourselves for discipleship to such a one? By no moral right, I am sure, but we nonetheless do want to be his disciples and most of us want to be worthy disciples. We want the church that bears his name to deserve the name it bears. Before we call ourselves or our church Christian, I suggest two questions growing out of the experience of our Lord. Is the church silent in the presence of grave problems? Can the church be silenced by those who are afraid or who do not want to bear the burden of her witness?

I think so often of what George MacLeod of Iona Community in Scotland once wrote,

121

I simply argue that the cross be raised again at the corner of the marketplace as well as on the steeple of the church. I am recovering the claim that Jesus was not crucified in a cathedral between two candles, but on a cross between two thieves; on the town garbage heap; at a crossroads so cosmopolitan that they had to write his title in Hebrew and in Latin and in Greek (or shall we say in English, in Bantu, and in Afrikaans?) ; at the kind of a place where cynics talk smut, and thieves curse, and soldiers gamble. Because that is where he died, and that is what he died about. And that is where churchmen should be, and what churchmen should be about.

The French have a story that sums up the matter in a very significant way. It seems that two angels had been off on divine business while our Lord had been on earth and had not seen what happened to him here. They saw him shortly after his return to heaven and asked him what had happened during his journey to earth. He told them how he had been born into the home of an artisan and had lived there most of his life before going into the public ministry; how he had been widely heard and loudly acclaimed at first, but how the crowds slipped away from him and the critics began to gather in numbers and power, finally agreeing to put him to death. They put him to death on the cross as a common criminal and after several agonizing hours he died. But God would not leave him among the dead and on the third day raised him and restored him to his rightful place, both on earth and in heaven. After hearing this recital, one angel exclaimed, "My Lord, was there no other way?" And he answered, "No. There was no other way."

Chapter 7

WHY DID HE LIVE AGAIN?

Scripture: I Corinthians 15:1-20

Text
"But in fact Christ has been
raised from the dead."
(*I Cor. 15:20*)

Friend and foe alike thought it was over—all over—when they put him in the tomb. They were certain that whatever, if anything, had begun and continued in him during his public ministry had come to a full and complete stop when the stone was rolled across the entrance to the tomb made available by Joseph of Arimathea. They thought it was over—but the story had just begun! What to them was an ending was to God the beginning.

I

As happens so often in less climactic ways, when we give up, God is just beginning. When, so far as we can see, we have come to a blank wall across the road, God finds and opens a door so that the journey, his and ours, may continue. That is the permanent glory of the festival season which Christians celebrate on Easter. As the Passover celebrates the deliverance of the Jewish community from slavery to freedom, Easter has come to be a celebration of the deliverance of all men from sin and death through the power of God in Jesus Christ.

The temptation simply to celebrate the triumph of Easter is almost irresistable. So we feel it today, and so they felt it in the New Testament. Paul's firm word is true to every page of that book: "But in fact Christ has been raised from the dead." As we read in it anywhere, we discover that the lines Emily Dickinson once penned about a spring day apply even more truly to it:

> The only news I know
> Is bulletins all day
> From Immortality.[1]

Yet we must do more than simply celebrate. We must seek to understand; we must base our celebration on

[1] "The Only News I Know." Copyright 1929, © 1957 by Mary L. Hampson. From *The Complete Poems of Emily Dickinson,* ed. by Thomas H. Johnson, by permission of Little, Brown and Co.

understanding—if it is to bear fruit. We cannot pretend that we have come to grips with the message of Jesus Christ either for New Testament times or our own unless we take full and serious account of the climactic claims of the Christian gospel: Death did not put an end to him or to the gospel! I know of no historian who has ever tried to account for the origin of the Christian church apart from the experience and the word which raced among the incredulous disciples on the third day after the death of Jesus: "We have seen the Lord." While I do not think it necessary to make the extreme claim that there is nothing of value in the New Testament except this belief, it is true to fact to say that every important thing in the New Testament is inseparably related to it. There would have been no church in New Testament times without it; nor would there be one today worth the name "Christian" without it. These facts suggest why we must deal with the question, "Why did he live again?" as the concluding theme in our study of "The Mind of Christ."

II

As we deal with it, we need to remind ourselves of the proper relationship between the first Christians and the books of the New Testament. The first Christians had not a book, not even a line of the book we treasure as the New Testament today. They were bound into a fellowship by their own experiences of the power of God in Christ, by the recollections of what Jesus had said and done, and by the great commission given to each and every one of them to take the gospel to the ends of the earth. These experiences, recollections, and the commission both knit them into a fellowship and provided the materials out of which our New Testament—and many other books now lost—grew.

The church—the Christian community, the fellowship of believers in Christ—came first. It was a contagious and powerful reality before there was a body of writings called the New Testament. This early community was knit together by a common experience of fellowship with a living Christ from the day of his resurrection in A.D. 29 or 30. The New Testament came inevitably out of this fellowship. People who had not known Jesus asked of those who had, what he said and did, who was with him, and a thousand other questions that would make him more real to them. But it took time—nearly a hundred years—for these experiences to find their way into the New Testament as we have it today.

We are able to say with some confidence that the New Testament grew through four stages.

Assuming that Jesus was crucified in A.D. 30, the first period running from A.D 30 to 50 was one of intense missionary activity and rough organization of the life and work of the church. It was in this period of twenty years that oral traditions and scattered jottings of the disciples were taking form. Practically all we know about this period comes to us from the book of Acts, the full title of which is "The Acts of the Apostles," meaning men such as Peter, Paul, Barnabas, Luke, and many others.

During the second period, from A.D. 50 to 60, the first books of our New Testament—the letters of Paul— were written. They reflect the vigorous growth and spread of the Christian church all over the Mediterranean world. During the third period, from A.D. 60 to 75, the Gospels of Mark, Luke, and Matthew endeavored to present the life of our Lord in a systematic form. During the fourth period, from A.D. 90 to 125, the Gospel of John and probably all other books in the New Testament were written.

When I say the early church produced or wrote the New Testament, I do not mean that it made an effort to produce one sharply consistent account of the life of Jesus. If that had been done, we would have one Gospel instead of four; we would have one source of information about the Resurrection instead of five—for we must include the book of Acts on this matter. The church treasured the fullest, most accurate, most credible accounts of him. It was utterly unconcerned about the discrepancies in the several accounts of his birth, crucifixion, and resurrection. It was enough for them that he had been born, killed, and lived again—and had commissioned them to take the gospel to the ends of the earth.

We live at a time nearly two thousand years removed from the days of Jesus' death and resurrection. We are completely dependent on the New Testament records for any account of what happened then, as well as why it happened. For that reason, I suggest we must give close attention to the New Testament witness to the resurrection of our Lord.

The four Gospels not only give us a united witness to the fact that death could not contain Jesus Christ, but they also acquaint us with different versions of the experiences of the disciples on the first Easter Day. They may and do disagree on who went to the tomb, who got there first, and what was said, but there is not the slightest shadow of disagreement on the great central claim of Easter: Jesus rose from the dead. His resurrection—in some form—was accepted and presented as fact.

If space permitted, a comparative and systematic study of the ways in which the four Gospels tell of this pivotal event would be very rewarding. But now we must content ourselves with a quick look and the simple fact that, however differently they may account for it, there is unbroken agreement in the claim that the powerful love of God had brushed aside the death and burial of Jesus Christ and had restored him to the disciples' company as their appointed and eternal leader.

Mark, the first Gospel to be written, comes to us with not one but two concluding sections, each of which contains an account of what happened at the tomb. In the first one, three women, Mary Magdalene, Mary, the mother of James, and Salome came to the tomb to cover his body with spices. As they approached, they were worrying about who would roll away the stone so that they might enter. But the stone was already rolled away; they entered and saw the angel who told of the Resurrection and asked them to go tell the disciples about it. "And they went out and fled from the tomb; for trembling and astonishment had come upon them; and they said nothing to anyone, for they were afraid." (16:8)

The second ending of Mark is quite different.

Now when [Jesus] rose early on the first day of the week, he appeared first to Mary Magdalene. . . . She went and told those who had been with him. . . . But when they heard that he was alive and had been seen by her, they would not believe it. After this he appeared in another form to two of them as they were walking into the country. . . . Afterward he appeared to the eleven themselves as they sat at table; and he upbraided them for their unbelief and hardness of heart, because they had not believed those who saw him after he had risen. (16:9-14)

So much for Mark.

Matthew had Mark's account before him as he wrote, and he embraced the second ending in which he made a number of changes. He has two Marys—Mary Magdalene and the other Mary—go to the tomb. He has a great earthquake: "For an angel of the Lord descended from heaven and came and rolled back the stone, and sat upon it. . . . For fear of him the guards trembled and became like dead men." (28:2-4) The angel told the women what to do and they ran to tell the disciples. "And, behold, Jesus met them (the disciples) and said, 'Hail!' And they came up and took hold of his feet and worshiped him." (28:9) Then Matthew adds the story of the sealing of the tomb by the chief priest and the attempt to bribe the guards to say that his disciples had stolen his body while they slept.

Luke, with Mark and other sources before him, has his own version of the experiences of Easter Morn. "The women who had come with him from Galilee," (23:55) including "Mary Magdalene and Joanna and Mary the mother of James," (24:10) were the ones who came to the tomb. "And they found the stone rolled away from the tomb, but when they went in they did not find the body." Then "Two men . . . in dazzling apparel" appeared suddenly and explained what had happened. The women "returning from the tomb . . . told all this to the eleven and to all the rest. . . . . But these words seemed to [the apostles] an idle tale, and they did not believe them." (24:1-12)

Then Luke gives us the warmly human story of the appearance of Jesus on the road to Emmaus with two disciples neither of whom belonged to the eleven central disciples. These two ran to Jerusalem and told the eleven of their experience with him. And as they were telling it, Jesus himself appeared.

John gives us a startlingly different version from these. Mary Magdalene came alone to the tomb. When she discovered that the stone had been rolled away, she ran back to the disciples and reported that someone had stolen Jesus' body from the tomb. Peter and another disciple hurried with Mary back to the tomb. The two men entered and discovered that it was empty. Then the men returned to their homes. But not Mary.

[She] stood weeping outside the tomb, and as she wept, she stooped to look into the tomb; and she saw two angels in white, sitting where the body of Jesus had lain. . . . They said to her, "Woman, why are you weeping?" She said to them, "Because they have taken away my Lord, and I do not know where they have laid him." [Then, as she turned to leave, she saw someone else whom she supposed to be the gardner.] She said to him, "Sir, if you have carried him away, tell me where you have laid him, and I will take him away." Jesus said to her, "Mary." (20:11-16)

She recognized him and cried aloud in joy and adoration. At his command, she went to the disciples and told them what had happened.

John continues by saying that later that same day Jesus appeared to the disciples and convinced them, especially Thomas, that he was actually alive. Still later he appears to them in Galilee and puts Peter to the test, telling him to "Feed my sheep."

We must add to this impressive witness of the four Gospels to the Resurrection experiences, others found in the book of Acts. Luke, the author, begins by saying that Jesus "presented himself alive after his passion by many proofs, appearing to [the apostles] during forty days." (1:3) Peter makes the point over and over again in three sermons attributed to him in the opening chapters of the book of Acts: "But God raised him up, having loosed the pangs of death, because it was not possible for him to be held by it." (2:24)

One of the earliest and most complete listings of the appearances of Jesus following the resurrection is found in Paul's first letter to the Corinthians—written, let us remember, before the Gospels were written. According to Paul, Jesus appeared to Peter, to the twelve, to "More than five hundred brethren at one time, most of whom are still alive," to James, to all the apostles, and finally to Paul himself on the road to Damascus. (15:4-8) This record by Paul is most impressive. He is saying to the doubters among the Corinthians. "Many people—still living—saw the Risen Lord, and here are their names. Ask them about it." John Knox writes, "The primitive Christian community was not a memorial society with its eyes fastened on a departed master; it was a dynamic community created around a living and present Lord." [2]

[2] *Jesus, Lord and Christ* (New York: Harper & Row, 1958). p. 118.

At the risk of laboring an obvious point, let it be emphasized that the early church did not believe in the Risen Lord because of these records; *it wrote these records out of its own widely and deeply felt experience of fellowship with the Risen Lord.* The experience preceded and called forth the records which we now cherish as our New Testament. Later generations such as our own might move from the written word to the living experience, but not in the early church. For most of them "it was rather that he was known to have risen because he was known as living." [3] The heart of the faith that brought and bound them together was the conviction that "death could not hold him, that, as Paul says, "in fact, Christ has been raised from the dead." Read the New Testament with this in mind and you discover that it "is quite as sure that Jesus still lives —or lives again—as that he lived at all." [4]

Does all this strike us as it did some of those who first heard it as "an idle tale"? Much in it does smack of folk versions of an important event—a rank growth of wishes, hopes, and dreams, unpruned by rational and careful thought. And, let it be admitted, there is much of that in our New Testament accounts. But there is more—much more than that. There is the firm witness that death could not conquer the love of God.

[3] *Ibid.*, p. 120.
[4] *Ibid.*, p. 119.

Jesus Christ was more than the winsome, powerful teacher and prophetic reformer the disciples told about; he was their Lord and Savior. In him—the risen, living Lord—they had found forgiveness of sins and their assurance of life eternal. He had conquered sin and death, and through him they shared in the victory. This had been Paul's experience on the road to Damascus fifteen years before he wrote his first letter to the Thessalonians, twenty years before he wrote to the Corinthians, and thirty years before the first Gospel was written. For him and for all of the first Christians, the experience of fellowship with the living Christ came first; the records of it which we call the New Testament came later as expressions of, and witnesses to, it. As we study this experience in the New Testament, we find our answer to the question, "Why did he live again?"

III

He lived again because God raised him from the dead.

God was working a mighty work of redemption and reconciliation through Jesus Christ—a work that was greater and more powerful than sin and death. Easter proved the truth of what Jesus had felt to be true all through his public ministry: The kingdom of God which he inaugurated was more important than life and far more powerful than death. He felt the pulse of eternity both in his call and in his work. "I work—and my Father worketh in me," he said. "What I do must

135

go on, and you must do it. Death cannot touch me or the work or those who prove true to the task."

He lived again because the purpose of God which called him into the public ministry and sustained him through it required the continuation of his power and presence among his disciples.

God needed him, not as a dead prophet or a martyred saint, but as a glorious, living leader of those who were carrying out the great commission to preach the gospel of the kingdom of love to the ends of the earth. From where we sit, this might look impossible, but from where God sits, it was necessary. In and through Jesus Christ he was inaugurating a new kingdom—a kingdom of love. Inaugurating is the word: not a finished and final achievement handed man on a celestial platter by means of a miracle, but both a vision and demonstration of what that kingdom means in Jesus Christ. It has never been enough to say that when we see Jesus Christ, we see God. The full fact is this: When we see him, we see God's will for the world and for our own lives. That will is the creation of a kingdom of love, first, within us as worthy citizens of it, then wherever our influence reaches as builders of it in the affairs of the world.

The glory of that vision of the love of God as we see it in Christ is beyond belief. Once we glimpse it, once we feel its power and its purpose, we who are earth-born are no longer earth-bound. This freeing of people like us from the paralyzing clutch of life as it is and giving us a new chance at finding and following God's will for our lives—this, I say, is the work of God in Christ. And it is a continuing, unending work. Only the experience of a living leader and guide can keep it alive in the hearts of men. Only if Christ be that living presence in our lives can the kingdom of God become a reality for us and through us. Without him, we would soon cut the kingdom of God down to our size. Instead of growing to fit it, we would shrink it to fit us. We would rationalize it until it was little more than our way of life, gloried, magnified and deified as a magnificent idol before which we would ask the world to bow. Only as we are able to keep clearly before us the vision of God's will in Christ will we be able to keep the kingdom and ways of this world in proper perspective and under the creative judgment of that which far transcends anything we have ever known or dreamed.

Jesus Christ not only inaugurated the kingdom of God as a living force and fact in history, but he alone is capable of keeping it that. With him it lives; without him it dies. And if it should die, man's last and greatest hope for himself and his future is gone. But since the first Easter we no longer fear or think of death as an ultimate power. Love alone is the ultimate power— and before it death bows as a loyal subject. Since Resurrection Morn, we have known, though we have not always followed in faith, that love is the most powerful force on earth because it is of God. Only as we believe that will we be able to keep at the endlessly difficult task of being those through whom love may find effective utterance and creative expression in our day.

God in his wisdom saw that those who would serve in the building of this kingdom required the living presence of, and deep personal fellowship with, the one whose life and teachings made that kingdom a vital reality, a real alternative. Before he came, men spoke of the kingdom as belonging to what Alice might call "the never, never world"; but since and because he lived his life on earth, it has been a here-and-now world in which human life and relationships can and ought to be transformed through love. We can be effective Christians only so long as we are conscious of our fellowship with the living Christ. That is why on Easter Day we concentrate not on the lilies of the field, which he loved, but upon him through whom all life flames up with new radiance and new meaning. In him—as nowhere else—we see, we feel, we know the meaning of God. Paul's word still holds for us: We are called to be "ambassadors for Christ." We are called to be the ones through whom God speaks this word of redeeming love.

No man would claim to be worthy of this calling—but, worthy or no, it is the heritage of every confessing Christian. Nothing less than fellowship with the living Christ can enable us to be the ambassadors of whom

Paul speaks. Not for anything less or other than that—but for that alone are we in the Christian church. We are the ones through whom the word of love which God speaks in Christ continues to be spoken today. "God making his appeal through me." But "who is sufficient for this?" For this high calling we need fellowship with him of whom God said, "This is my beloved son . . . in whom I am well pleased."

John Stuart Mill once said, "The world needs to be reminded that such a one as Socrates once lived." Having loved and studied the wise old Greek master for more than thirty-five years, I would agree. But this I know: There is something more important than that. This world needs to be reminded of one who lived and died at the hands of people such as us and, by the grace of God, lived again and walks the highways of the world as guide and strength to every willing soul in the human family. And though he picks us up at widely different points on the compass of life, the longer we walk with him, the closer we come together until, by the grace of God, our separateness is swallowed up in the togetherness of the love of God which makes us one.

How well we can understand the Mexican matador, El Cordobes, who, when asked if he were afraid of death, said, "No. Only life scares me."

Nothing less than the power of the living God can nerve people such as us to the living of these days and, even more, to the holy task of being ambassadors for

Christ in a world such as this. For sin must be faced and called by its right name: a conscious violation of the will of God. We must face it in ourselves, in our churches, in our world. And we must find somehow the power to overcome it. Paul found this power in Christ, through whom he said we could be more than conquerors of all that might face us.

If Paul was right—and I am sure he was—we can be more than conquerors of hatred, prejudice, and anger. We can be more than conquerors of conflict between classes, races, and nations. But the conquest will not be easy. It cannot be won by words alone. But the victory can and must come in lives, churches, and communities such as ours—and, God strengthen us, in a world like this! And it must come in terms of new purposes, new goals, new communities, new laws, until it is possible for us to live in peace with one another and with God.

If Paul was right—and I am sure he was—we can be more than conquerors of death and the fear of death. In and through the providence of God death comes to all. But, thanks be to Christ, it no longer comes as an enemy or as the full end of life. Now it is a doorway framed by God's love and placed before us all. And as we step through it, the love of God which created us and created death moves with us to life eternal. Even as death could not contain him who is the incarnation of the love of God, it cannot contain the spirit of man which finds its birth, strength, and purpose in God.

Deeper and more lasting than the hundred and one questions, asked and unasked, which cluster around this faith is the faith itself that Christ burst the bonds of death and the fear of death and flung wide the doors of eternal life. He was, he is, and he will always be, a mighty word spoken from the heart of God to the heart of man, and nothing men do can silence him. Nearly a hundred years after his death and resurrection, John heard that word and cried, "In the beginning was the Word, and the Word was with God, and the Word was God. . . . And the Word became flesh and dwelt among us, full of grace and truth; we have beheld his glory, glory as of the only Son from the Father." (John 1:1, 14)

In Jesus Christ we are continually confronted and confounded by the meaning and the power of God!

Love is the most powerful force on earth: It, and it alone, can meet and master greed, lust, and hate.

Love can empower one to turn the other cheek, to go the second mile.

Love can enable one to identify himself with any man anywhere at the point of his deepest need.

Love alone can empower one to face the full fury of hate and vengeance with the prayer, "Father, forgive them for they know not what they do."

Love alone can confront death with the word, "Father, I trust my spirit in your hands."

Love and no lesser force can overcome death, can

reduce death from an ultimate fate to an unimportant fact about life.

And love has done all this, not in theory, but in fact, in Jesus Christ and to and for all who have faith in him.

This fact, then—fact about him and fact about our faith in him—we lift on high and cry: "Glory to God in the highest! In and through Jesus Christ his love reigns supreme!"

You may recall the moving words with which Arnold Toynbee, in *A Study of History,* closes his chapter on the false messiahs who have mislead the human spirit:

When we set out on this quest we found ourselves moving in the midst of a mighty host, but as we have pressed forward, the marchers, company by company, have fallen out of the race . . . until only the gods were left in the running. At the final ordeal of death, few, even of these would-be saviour gods, have dared to put their title to the test by plunging into the icy river. And now, as we stand and gaze with our eyes fixed upon the farther shore, a simple figure rises from the flood and straightway fills the whole horizon. There is the Saviour.

I am glad so distinguished a historian as Dr. Toynbee has put the Christian witness in so moving a way. But I would like to put it in the language of a five-year-old boy who was on his first ride on a transcontinental railroad. When the train plunged into the first tunnel and blackness enfolded all, the boy gasped in surprise. Suddenly the train cleared the tunnel and daylight took over again. The boy exclaimed, "It's tomorrow today!" In Jesus Christ we have always found it to be so: It is tomorrow today.